Response to *Rescue from Darkness*

"I can't think of a ministry that has informed my application of disciple making as effectively as D Expansion. For more than three decades I've ha.. ..,. .... watching this ministry identify and hone best practices for the benefit of kingdom workers around the world. Doug is presenting a second offering in discipleship making outlining the practical and essential discipline of prayer.. It amazes me how much we kingdom workers talk about prayer, but we don't embrace its power. For many prayer isn't the meat and potatoes, it is the garnish on the plate and that is to our detriment. There are profound blessings and opportunities when we pursue the power of prayer in disciple making. As Doug writes, you can be confident it comes not just from the world of the philosophical, but of the practical. The disciplines are time tested and fruitful. Doug is a friend, a mentor and an important voice in the work of reaching the nations."
Todd Bussey
Ministry Development Pastor
Christ's Church Ministries, Jacksonville, FL

"Upon being saved from darkness, Jesus often sends us back to the darkness to save others. Rescue from Darkness is a compelling invocation about the transformative power of prayer, coupled with biblical references and real-life examples, intended to encourage persistent and expectant prayer. It's a call to action, urging believers to prioritize prayer and pray for open doors and hearts for the Gospel. Rescue from Darkness is a hit."
Larrie Fraley
Lead Missions Pastor
Christ's Church of the Valley, Peoria, AZ

"Having known Doug for a few decades now and having seen him up close and personal in many situations, I can attest to the character of the man behind the stories in this book. Doug cares about lost people and has dedicated his life to living on mission for the kingdom! His lifetime of lessons will challenge you to live out your own faith and prayer life in deeper ways! I highly recommend this book."
Wade Landers, PhD
Ozark Christian College, Joplin, MO

"Doug Lucas has written a highly impactful, short-but-practical book that God can use to change the trajectory of our lives. He shares brief episodes from his amazing walk with Jesus, from God's Word, the role of prevailing prayer, and from Christian pastors/writers. We are to fully focus on Christ, on God's Kingdom to live solely for things eternal, for God's glory, for the multiplication of disciples. Doug shares life lessons and truths to challenge us to yield fully, to believe God and to fervently pray, to nurture a growing faith that causes us to hunger daily for God, His will and eternal Kingdom. He calls upon us to see beyond our passing trials and testings and to see God working radical changes in the lives of many others. He dares us not to waste our lives on passing/fleeting earthly matters when we are all called to make heavenly investments. Thank you Doug for sharing your life and for calling many others to be faithful, available stewards and laborers."
Dr. Jonathan Miller, MD, MPH

"Rescue from Darkness is a winsome book calling believers to be sold out in following Jesus. Doug weaves together an engaging mix of Scripture, incredible personal stories, motivating quotes, and practical steps. The title captures his double challenge – to engage in rescuing those out of darkness who have little access to Jesus and to draw believers out of the dim shadows of an aimless life into a bright place of hope, prayer, purpose, and action. I came away from this book asking myself if I was going to use the few remaining years of life in 'breeding spotted mice' (read the book to find out about this) or invest my days in eternity? Take up and read. You won't be disappointed."
Dan Scribner, Executive Director
Joshua Project, Colorado Springs, CO

"In this booklet, Doug Lucas shares a series of pivotal events which helped shape his life and ministry. It is a great example of how God takes each of us, as a bit of sand, and lovingly lays down layer upon layer of Himself on us until we become beautiful pearls. A bit of Doug's passion for the Lord and His Kingdom will surely rub off on you as you read these anecdotes."
Curtis Sergeant
A disciple of Jesus

RESCUE
FROM DARKNESS

DOUG LUCAS

MORE DISCIPLES
PUBLISHING

©Copyright 2023 by Team Expansion

Published by MORE DISCIPLES PUBLISHING
Cover and interior design by JC Williams

Unless indicated otherwise, all Scripture quotations in this publication are from the HOLY BIBLE, NEW INTERNATIONAL VERSION Copyright 1973, 1978, 1984 by International Bible Society. All rights reserved.

First Edition

ISBN: 979-8-87-823688-1

Acknowledgments

Thanks to Carla, Jonathan, Linda, Mary, Penny, and Tina, who patiently and carefully proofed the manuscript for this book. Thanks to JC for countless hours laying out the text and designing the cover. You make all things better. Most of all, thanks to God for His abundant grace and mercy.

Special Note from the Author and Publisher

After covering expenses, any and all proceeds from the sale of this book will be applied toward the costs of conducting disciple-making movement (DMM) trainings in locations worldwide.

Contents

1
Introduction

6
The Awesome Power of Hope

8
The Amazing Potential of Fruit

11
The Astonishing Preeminence of Prayer

14
He Can Rescue the Restricted: A Case Study

19
More Prayer: Our First Recourse

23
PUSH: Pray Until Something Happens

41
Make Your Calling Sure

48
Resilience Through Suffering

51
Your Mission, If You Decide to Accept It

55
A Strategy for Launching
Disciple-Making Movements (DMMs)

69
Epilogue

76
Addendum

Introduction

Truth is, my Dad was never very excited about me joining Boy Scouts. I was in fifth grade. We had a decent house, and I had a warm, soft bed. He could never figure out why I would want to go sleep on the hard ground inside a floor-less tent on a cold weekend in October. But, as dads sometimes do – he finally went along with it.

I was proud to be a part of Troop 516. But to be honest, some of the guys came from troubled homes and, frankly, some of them lived troubled lives. But I was trying to make the most of it. I think I had learned just enough about scouting to "be prepared," but not enough to know exactly **how**. During this weekend campout in a field just a bit west of Bedford, Indiana, we were supposed to go spelunking in Blue Springs Cavern, which was still "undeveloped." I didn't know quite what to expect. My mom and dad sent me with our "dry cell" flashlight. For those not old enough to remember, a "dry cell" flashlight is rather huge – larger than a 1/2-gallon paint can – and just as cumbersome. I also took my mom's ancient Brownie camera. (Why she trusted me with that camera I'll never understand.) And we all were supposed to bring a lunch. Mine was packed in a brown paper bag (of course). Fortunately, the camera case had a shoulder strap. Otherwise, I would have run out of hands.

When we arrived at the cave on that cold afternoon, I confess that the cave entrance gave me pause. They called this entrance, "The Chimney," but it was more like climbing down in a well. I'm sure it was probably only 10 or 15 feet, but it felt every bit like 30 to me. We had no ladder and no belay. (I don't even think I knew the word at the time.) We climbed down that "Chimney" one at a time and I somehow made it. We switched on our lights right away. It was **dark** down there. My "dry cell" battery must have been old. It was completely drained in 30 minutes. There were probably 30 or 40 of us on this particular tour. Wouldn't you know it, I was near the back of the single file line. The cave guide did have a nice "torch light" on his fancy caving helmet. But that blinding cave light was pointed forward. All I could make out was a ghoulish scene of 30 little fifth-grade heads bobbing up and down like silhouettes at a bad Halloween party.

As we walked deeper into that dark cave, there were times when I could hear rocks being knocked off the cave floor. There was apparently a deep gorge off to our right. The path grew narrower and wetter as we walked. As a fifth grader, I could just picture myself slipping on a wet stone in the dark, sliding off the ledge, and falling off the cliff to our right. Then the ceiling began lowering on us. It was a bit like being in a garbage compactor. The floor gradually became a stream, and we were finally wading through 4 inches of water. I hadn't worn the right shoes. (What would have been the right shoes for this?) There was a "Fat Man's Misery" (seems like every cave has one of those) and a "Duck Walk" – by this time, the height of the cave had dropped to around four feet. I was beginning to think my dad was right.

After around three hours of hiking, however, the cave finally opened up into an amazingly large room, large enough to be a small auditorium. The guide signaled that this was the spot for lunch break. I pretended to enjoy my soggy peanut butter sandwich until he finally looked at the guys around him and said, "OK, ready to start back?" My heart sank. "You mean, we have to walk back out the way we came in?" He muttered some comment about, "How else would we get out," but for some reason, I just had never contemplated we'd have to do all that again – three hours of duck-walking, wading, soggy boots, shivering lips, and scary, dark, muddy ledges. I was having a no-good-for-nothing-rotten day. But three hours later, we were back at The Chimney. Just when I thought the day was starting to look up, I did (look up) and someone bombed me with a snowball. While we were in the cave, it had snowed at least three inches. I could already feel the freezing cold as I tried to shinny up that crazy chimney. Once I made it up top, I was pelted with more snowballs. It was getting dark. And when we finally made it back to the campsite, there were our cold canvas tents, with no floors, and not a single stick of dry firewood.

I just stood there, looking into the tent while the other guys (the troubled ones) threw snowballs at one another.

That's when I heard my name. "Douglas Kevin, you get your things and get into this car!" It was my dad's voice. I turned around and there he was in that golden-brown Dodge Polara. (I tried to conceal the fact that nothing had ever looked more beautiful at that moment.) I grabbed my pack, shouted something over my head to the scoutmaster and literally **dove** into the back seat of that car – the very, very, very **warm** back seat.

For the longest time, no one said a word. Finally, I just softly said, "Thank you." All my dad said was, "I don't know why you wanted to sleep out in the cold anyway. You've got a warm bed at home." He was right. It was like a rescue from cold and darkness. And I've never forgotten it, nor will I for as long as I live.

The Apostle Paul wrote in Colossians 1:13, "For he has **rescued us from the dominion of darkness** and brought us into the kingdom of the Son he loves (NIV)." Back in fifth grade, it felt like the struggle was real. But now, as an adult, it seems, if anything, a bit worse. We live in tumultuous times. Wars, climate change, political polarity, and economic hardship have prompted well over 100 million people to run away from their homes and families – more than ever before in all recorded history. Worldviews are changing so rapidly that we can barely keep up with the shifting sands. A vast global pandemic seems to have shaken up some of our long-held personal moorings. Despite being brought up in the church, many of today's young people have reportedly just walked away. Many have come to doubt the very existence of God Himself.

The darkness is everywhere, but it seems like everyone has a story of being rescued from it. In the opening session of a recent planning retreat with Team Expansion's Leadership Team, I shared my Blue Springs Cavern story and then asked if anybody else had a story like that. To my absolute surprise, almost **everyone** did. One VP told of being stuck in a dark tent, alone. Another told of searching for his six-month-old baby on a series of staircases in the dark. It sounded like a bad, scary movie. Yet another told of her son complaining about any bright light one night while serving overseas – because he had contracted bacterial meningitis. Another told us of nearly losing his life while white-water rafting in West Virginia the weekend after a series of hard rains. (After being swept out of the boat by three different sets of rapids, he finally disembarked and called for a Jeep to come pick him up.) One leader told about having giant rocks thrown at her car in the middle of the night on a rugged African road. The same leader went on to describe being trapped in a dark room, just before she heard the gunshot that took the life of her husband. That same night, the thieves kidnapped her son. Fortunately, he was rescued that same night (from darkness), but **nobody** wants to live a night like that. Yet, this is our human condition. A kind of entropy drags us down into the darkness. A kind of inertia wants to hold us there as we struggle.

In the long thoughts of history and eternity, haven't we seen just this kind of maelstrom roar before? Somehow, we have convinced ourselves that these times are unique, forgetting past epochs of suffering, persecution, and lostness. At the end of the day, everything is relative. Any life can feel lost, just as any day brings with it certain darkness. The Good News is that Christ came to rescue us from **all darkness**, both temporal and eternal. That rescue brings with it hope and help for today, as well as the promise of light for tomorrow and all time.

The chorus sums it up for all of us:

> I want to be in the Light
> As You are in the Light
> I want to shine like the stars in the heavens
> Oh, Lord be my Light and be my salvation
> Cause all I want is to be in the Light
> All I want is to be in the Light

(The words were actually written by a songwriter/producer named Charlie Peacock. But for many of us, dcTalk made them famous on their album, "Jesus Freak.")

Believers who seek to share the Good News with others today can therefore do so with boldness and authority. Prayer has a unique power to open doors and provide lift for individuals, communities, and cultures. When practiced humbly and openly, prayer overcomes barriers and restrictions like no other Christian practice. In addition, it can confirm callings, provide relief from suffering, and open one's mind and heart to the true impact of the Word of God itself.

Make no mistake: prayer is not our sole strategy for making disciples. But in light of everything we're learning about God, movements, and mankind, it should always be our first recourse.

Thus, a book about our "rescue from darkness" is actually, more than anything else, a book about Christ and the power of prayer. Sorting out these starting points can open the door to Kingdom movements like nothing else on earth. Join us, therefore, in pursuit of discovering hope, fruit, and the preeminence of prayer.

Chapter 1
THE AWESOME POWER OF HOPE

Colossae was an ancient city located in what is now Turkey. Although there is no evidence that Paul ever visited the city in person, he was still thankful for the faith of the believing community there. He begins his biblical letter to the Colossians by pointing out that he had heard of their faith and their "love that sprang from the **hope** stored up for them up in heaven" (Colossians 1:4-5). As a result, he thanked God for them.

Hope is a powerful force. It seems to be in short supply these days.

Some years ago, I remember hearing of a lab experiment involving some not-so-fortunate mice. In a research project that I'm sure would never be sanctioned by animal lovers, the researchers placed half of the mice in a glass-encased aquarium, which they then flooded with water. They counted down the seconds until the mice drowned. (As I mentioned, the People for the Ethical Treatment of Animals would never have approved of this study.) In the second half of the study, the researchers painted a door in the top of the glass aquarium. Keep in mind, the door wasn't even real, but it **resembled** the door in the top of the cage where the mice had been living prior to their ill-fated involvement in the project. Researchers placed the other half of the mice in this second container with the door, then flooded this aquarium with water as well. In this instance, the mice lived at least **twice** as long before they drowned. The whole time, they were pawing and scratching at the image of the door in the top of the aquarium, leading the researchers to conclude that **hope** is life-giving, powerful enough even to sustain life itself – at least for a while.

Although I was not able to verify the source (or the veracity) of this story (the lab was probably shut down for cruelty to animals), I have never forgotten the lesson – hope can lift us beyond imagined limits. Hope can empower us well beyond human capabilities. Believers in Colossae had discovered hope in the gospel of Christ Jesus. Frankly, we could use a little of this hope today.

When Jesus rescues us from darkness, it not only brings promise of a hope in the life beyond, but it offers hope in the current life, too.

Chapter 2
THE AMAZING POTENTIAL OF FRUIT

In his letter to the believers in Colossae, Paul went on to draw attention to the fact that "the gospel was bearing fruit and growing through the whole world" (Colossians 1:6). In fact, the community of followers in Colossae were living proof of Kingdom expansion. He explains in Colossians 1:9 that, for this reason, he had not stopped praying for them. In verse 11, he encouraged them to take strength and power from God's glorious might so that they might have endurance and patience. While still rejoicing for them as "fruit of the Gospel," he dared them to find joy in the fact that, through God's mercy, God had qualified them "to share in the inheritance of his holy people in the kingdom of light" (verse 12).

Fruit is an encouraging sign, especially when it stems from mercy provided by God Himself.

College, for me, was a bit like *A Tale of Two Cities* (by Charles Dickens): "It was the best of times, it was the worst of times." I was thankful for the provision of a full-ride scholarship: tuition, housing, food, books, and even supplies were all provided as long as I kept up a straight-A grade-point average.

By God's grace, I finished the entire four years with only one B+ – in Physical Education. I remember the day I couldn't jump quite high enough to reach the mark on the wall that would have let me skate by with an A-minus. It was so deflating. My classmates just couldn't quite believe it. I was this guy who was seemingly more motivated than anyone else in the gym – yet was unable to "reach the mark."

But I'll never forget one fellow student. His name was Bryan. He could pick up any sport – it didn't matter what it was. As long as there was a ball or net involved, he pretty much dominated it. When the gym instructor would appoint captains to pick teams, he would always choose Bryan as a captain. And when Bryan started picking his team, he would always choose me as his first pick. Me – the guy who couldn't even get an "A" in Phys. Ed. I couldn't jump high enough to reach that crazy mark on the wall. But Bryan always picked me first.

Confounded and confused, I finally just pulled him aside one day as he called me "Leapin' Lucas" from the other side of the gym. "Bryan," I asked humbly, "You always seem to pick me first, in spite of the fact that there are dozens of other guys in the gym who are more athletic, more gifted, and more skilled in just about any sport we ever tackle. Why in the world would you want to choose me first?"

He answered without a single moment of hesitation. "You're Leapin' Lucas. It's true you might not be the best at any of the sports we play, but you somehow have this way of making us care about the outcome – more so than anyone else in the entire class. When the rest of us are tempted to sit around and rest on our laurels, we see you working your heart out for the team and it makes us all better."

"Thanks, I think," I answered with a chuckle. Apparently, there's more to winning than meets the eye. At least according to Bryan, it takes not only athleticism, skill and gifting, but also, some sheer will. According to Bryan, caring begets more caring. Zeal inspires zeal. It's a kind of fruit that inspires more fruit.

I still haven't forgotten Bryan's life lesson. Momentum often is the direct result of a mass of weight being thrown in a particular direction. The mass doesn't have to be pretty. It just has to be launched. Momentum matters. Inertia matters. Fruit matters. The more fruit we see, the more excited we become.

For example, we sometimes receive calls from churches that have decided to support the work of a particular missionary because the church might have heard that, in that particular field, there have been many baptisms. Fruit matters. And fruit begets more fruit.

Paul was excited about the growth that was happening "throughout the whole world." He wrote that "the gospel is bearing fruit," just as it had been doing since the people in Colossae heard about it. These people in Colossae were serious about their faith. And Paul was thankful for them.

The Amazing Potential of Fruit

When Jesus rescues us from darkness, we represent a kind of fruit. And, as is the case with momentum, the exciting thing about fruit is that fruit begets more fruit.

Chapter 3
THE ASTONISHING PREEMINENCE OF PRAYER

The driving force of the entire first chapter of Colossians is prayer. Paul circles back to this all-important topic in the conclusion of the book, as well. "Devote yourselves to prayer," he exhorts (Col. 4:2). In doing so, he challenges them to be both "watchful and thankful." But much of Paul's life was focused on mission. At the core of these important concluding remarks, he asks them to pray that "God may open a door" for his message. He pleads with the community of believers in Colossae to pray that he might proclaim the message clearly, as he should (Col. 4:4).

Interestingly, when Paul wrote these words, he was imprisoned for his faith. Yet, he doesn't ask the Colossians to pray for better prison food. He doesn't even request prayer for his release! Instead, after being tossed in jail for speaking the message of Christ, he asks them to pray harder that he can share the Good News even more boldly and effectively. What kind of guy does that?

By now, probably all of us have heard of David Garrison's landmark studies on church-planting movements (CPMs). As the last century came to a close, Dr. Garrison began to notice that, in a dozen or more instances around the world, certain people were coming to Christ in droves. There were so many new disciples in those exceptional situations that he set about to look for commonalities that might have precipitated them.

While researching some two dozen instances of Kingdom movements – vast responses to Christ that had taken place in a fairly well-defined geographical location – he found that every single one of them had been preceded by a season of intensive prayer on the part of the team of witnesses seeking to launch the movement. But this was not ordinary two-minute praying. These teams of witnesses had prayed in the most fervent way for the most determined period of time Garrison had ever seen. He concluded that – to see a new Kingdom movement of people coming to Christ, one or more people needed to pray in an extraordinary way throughout a very intensive and intentional season. Extraordinary prayer had preceded every movement he discovered.

Garrison's findings prompted additional prayer on the part of those who had been seeking to launch new movements in other locations around the world. Now, some 25 years later, researchers have catalogued over 2,000 movements that have broken out following Garrison's initial studies. Over 100 million people have gotten involved. At first, some locations seemed tougher than others, but by the year 2020, Kingdom movements had broken out on every continent and in almost every country. Christianity has sprung up in almost every political landscape, and every unique country.

However, just as Paul wrote in 1 Corinthians 6:34, "there are some who are ignorant of God." Paul hastened to add, "I speak this to your shame." In his book, *A Third of Us*, researcher Marvin J. Newell writes that roughly 1/3 of the world's population still resides in a place where they can't get access to read or hear the Gospel even if they tried. Sadly, they have little hope for the current life and no tangible reason to hope for the next one. They haven't heard the Gospel because they are locked in a system that restricts the **sharing** of the Gospel. The religions of Islam, Hinduism, and atheism are such that proponents of those religions are on a mission to prevent other messages from permeating their societies. By doing so, I'm sure they feel they are doing right, seeking to preserve what they feel would be the truth. Sadly, their actions only compound the blindness and inaccessibility to the Gospel. Their people are **imbedded** in unreached people groups. They are **insulated** from the Gospel by barriers of language, culture, or societal norms. They live in **Gospel-restricted** locales. (See page 12 of *A Third of Us* for a complete explanation of these concepts.)

Although Jesus commanded us to make disciples of all nations, due in part to the difficulties we encounter in sharing Christ, we have become distracted by perfecting the saints in nations where people mostly already have access. This is a good work, to be sure. But, with so many people still without access, it feels like we're selling out to the whole "make disciples of all nations" thing (Matthew 28:19-20).

This is especially poignant in view of those Kingdom Movements mentioned above. In other words, in many cases, when someone starts extraordinary prayer, God chooses to act in spite of years of previous neglect. Entire waves of people come to Christ in some of the most unlikely places.

When Jesus rescues us from darkness, He begins answering our prayers. And seemingly, what most excites Him is answering prayers for the lost. God is truly the Lord of the Harvest.

Chapter 4
HE CAN RESCUE THE RESTRICTED: A CASE STUDY

So how does prayer transform an unreached people group into a Kingdom movement? It usually starts small. For example, throughout the late 1980s, countless prayer groups were asking God for help and understanding regarding how to penetrate what was then called the Soviet Union (the USSR) with the love of Christ. Many of us prayed for miracles – but few of us knew how to pray or exactly **what** to pray. The people of the USSR were, in many ways, shrouded in mystery. The government, which we all generally called "Russia," had imposed the most severe restrictions of our time.

Little by little, we began to see cracks in the wall, one brick at a time. We would hear about massive and dire food shortages, which prompted restlessness and, in some cases, even rebellion. The Chernobyl power station in Ukraine exploded in April 1986, giving the impression that Soviet powers were reeling. Mikhail Gorbachev had come to power as the head of the USSR in 1985. He was young and seemingly more idealistic. Soon there were protests in Poland, and finally, partially free elections in 1989. Other lands, emboldened by Poland's progress, began following similar paths. Eventually, East Germans flocked to the streets by the thousands. The Berlin Wall crumbled in November of 1989.

At the time, in addition to leading a mission organization, I was teaching part-time in a seminary in Cincinnati, Ohio. A mild-mannered fellow professor would walk by my desk every day, jokingly asking, "When are you going to send your first team to the Soviet Union?" I would respond with a nervous chuckle until one day, he stopped and said, "No – I'm serious."

I remember placing a call to an agency that very day that

had specialized in smuggling Bibles and relief into the USSR. I managed to get through to the head of that agency. He promptly reminded me how little I knew about it all and, with a somewhat dismissive tone, suggested I leave the work to him and his people. Discouraged, I recoiled inside my shell for a while – but continued to pray (as did many others).

One day, I heard about a special congress in Moscow that would explore options for sharing Good News among unreached people groups. None of us was even sure such a thing would be legal. The USSR was, after all, still the USSR. Nevertheless, I filled out the application to attend the meeting and was flatly rejected. "You haven't been to Russia. You don't speak Russian. You don't even appear to **know** any Russians. This congress will consist of 1,000 delegates from all across the Soviet Union. In addition to those Soviet delegates, we're inviting a carefully selected group of 100 guest participants from the entire rest of the world. We're so sorry, but you just aren't qualified." I was disappointed, but I saw their point. (They were right; I didn't even **know** any Russians, after all.)

Still, people prayed. And I prayed – hard. I reasoned that we had to get started **somewhere.** To me, this Lausanne congress, sponsored by Lausanne, was the perfect place. At the same time, I had to admit I could see the logic behind the approach the meeting's organizers had chosen to follow.

But the mild-mannered professor kept encouraging me onward. Other friends picked up the baton, saying they were praying too. So with great fear and trepidation, I began sending faxes to the organizing office. (Yes, we were still using the fax machine in 1989.) For months, I sent requests and letters, all written in the most humble way possible. One day in 1990, on the phone with the coordinating office, the administrator admitted that the office had been struck by my determination. They had a heart for my plea. They gave me the name of the head of the selection committee and encouraged me to pray for wisdom for him as he made his decision **that night** regarding exactly which non-Soviets would be invited. Yikes. I knew this was the moment.

We all prayed hard, but nothing happened. Around midnight that night (Eastern Time), the thought occurred to me that sometimes, while praying, it's important to **wait**. Other times,

He Can Rescue the Restricted: A Case Study | 15

while praying, it's important to **act.** I called Directory Assistance. (For those who know only Google, Directory Assistance was a giant office full of operators who would look up telephone numbers in other cities. I know. It was such a quaint system.) Somehow, I managed to track down the number for the head of the selection committee. His name was Bill. It was well after midnight, Eastern Time, by the time I called – so after 9 pm his time on the West Coast. To my absolute shock and surprise, he picked up the call.

"Is this the Bill who is acting as the head of the selection committee for the Moscow Congress on Evangelization of the USSR," I asked. After a very pregnant pause, he finally answered, "Yes, it is, but who is this?" I told him my name and, almost instantly, he answered, "Wait! Is this the guy who continues to send faxes to our office, asking to be invited to the Congress?" Yikes. I softly answered with one small yes.

He spoke sternly. "How many times do we have to tell you? This congress is not for beginners. Please, stop pestering us."

I answered calmly, yet more intentionally, "But I had to call and tell you that, I've been praying, and well, have you ever heard of the parable of the Widow and the Unjust Judge in Luke 18? I'm calling to say, I'm like the widow."

There was a long pause again. "And what does that make me?!" There was an awkward pause again. (I still can't believe I actually said that I was the widow.) Then suddenly, I could hear another voice in the background, speaking to Bill on the other end of the call. He finally came back and said, "Look, Mr. Lucas. My wife is here. She's been hearing this entire thing. She's saying that, if we're going to make a difference in Soviet Union, it will require a kind of unabashed, shameless audacity – a near coon-dog determination. I just want to ask: If we invite you to this congress, would you please work very hard not to embarrass me?" I pledged that I would work **incredibly** hard for that very thing.

The next day, they faxed me the invitation.

Jesus actually spoke of shameless audacity concerning prayer: the Friend at Midnight (Luke 11:5-8). Unless I'm wrong, in this parable, Jesus is actually encouraging courageous boldness on the part of those praying. See for yourself:

Then Jesus said to them, "Suppose you have a friend, and you go to him at midnight and say, 'Friend, lend me three

> loaves of bread; a friend of mine on a journey has come to me, and I have no food to offer him.' And suppose the one inside answers, 'Don't bother me. The door is already locked, and my children and I are in bed. I can't get up and give you anything.' I tell you, even though he will not get up and give you the bread because of friendship, yet because of your shameless audacity, (Or yet to preserve his good name) he will surely get up and give you as much as you need. "So I say to you: Ask and it will be given to you; seek and you will find; knock and the door will be opened to you. For everyone who asks receives; the one who seeks finds; and to the one who knocks, the door will be opened."

To me, the message behind this parable is clearly, "Think outside the box." Put another way, it's as if Jesus is saying, "When you pray, dream big." Don't be shy. If your prayer is for a good cause, ask!

In the parable about the Widow and the Unjust Judge, I don't really think God is comparing Himself to an 'unjust judge.' But maybe He is indeed trying to tell us something about Godly determination in prayer. Although I don't totally get it, it seems like He values tenacity and determination, as we humbly plead on our knees in prayer. Think about all the times we see verses like, "Always pray and don't faint" (Luke 18:1), "Never stop praying" (1 Thess. 5:17), and "Always keep on praying" (Eph. 6:18).

By the way, at the congress in Moscow, while talking with a researcher about where our mission organization should start in the USSR (if at all), a member of a visiting choir kept pestering me, asking me to come to visit his church in the very southern portion of the USSR. The more I tried to wave him off, the more determined he seemed to be. Finally, after I had tried to explain to him that our organization was focused on unreached people groups (not existing churches), he walked away. At that very moment, a light bulb went off in the researcher's head. The location of the church just happened to be 3 hours away from the homeland of the most strategic unreached people groups that the congress was promoting. I scrambled away to find the choir member and, within hours of wrapping up the congress, flew south with him to visit the region and the unreached group.

He Can Rescue the Restricted: A Case Study | 17

Months later, my family and I ended up moving to the area along with several other Team Expansion workers. Over the years that followed, God raised up a movement there consisting of scores of new churches and hundreds of new believers. The choir member's church became our partner. Team Expansion ended up working with others to oversee the translation of the Bible into a Muslim group's native language. We felt as if we were watching God at work throughout the entire experience – and He had given us a front-row seat.

Many partners have since participated in a journey that is still unfolding today. You see, the city where we worked was located in what is now modern-day Ukraine. The church and its staff have stepped up to the plate in a big way to help the people of their city endure incredible suffering in the current invasion they are experiencing. We are still partnering with them today. In some ways, the partnership is bigger than it has ever been before.

God rocks. He has the most uncanny ability to tie together dozens of loose ends and make amazing things happen – when we pray.

When Jesus rescues us from darkness, He seemingly wants to send us right back into the darkness to rescue others. Praying for those others seems to empower the entire process.

Chapter 5
MORE PRAYER: OUR FIRST RECOURSE

A few years ago, I wrote a book titled, *More Disciples*. When I began talking about **this** book, we considered the title, *More Prayer*. However, a wise-cracking friend quipped that I could then write a third volume in the series, *More Cowbell*. (Search YouTube for that title if you haven't seen the *Saturday Night Live* skit. On second thought, don't bother. [grin]) But the truth is, we do need to focus on more prayer, cowbells notwithstanding.

When friends came to Nehemiah to tell him about the fact that Jerusalem was lying in rubble, he listened intently (Neh. 1:3-4). The walls were down and its gates had been burned with fire. Nehemiah's reaction was heartfelt. He sat down and wept (Neh. 1:4). But his mourning then turned to fasting and prayer. As he prayed, God began to stir his heart (as God often does). Nehemiah was a wine taster at the time. The King trusted him a lot and noticed that Nehemiah was bummed about something. When the King asked what was up, the Bible is clear: Nehemiah prayed before he responded (Neh. 2:4). Not only did the King proceed to give Nehemiah permission to go back to Jerusalem to check it out personally, but in addition, the King sponsored his entire trip. What we need today is **more prayer**. We see this throughout multiple passages in the Word.

- James 5:16-18 – Prayer makes things happen. It "avails much."
- Exodus 32:7-14 – Apparently, prayers can even change God's mind!
- Isaiah 38:1-5 – Prayer can extend life.
- Acts 12:1-16 – Prayer can free captives who are in prison as a result of religious persecution.

- Philippians 4:6-7 – Prayer can help us find peace in the middle of anxious times.
- Acts 4:24-33 – Prayer can give us more boldness to share the Good News. (There's another title in the book series: *More Boldness*.)
- Matthew 9:38 – Prayer can raise up new workers for the harvest, then send them out.
- Luke 11:9-10 – Prayer can reveal God's will.
- James 1:5 – Prayer can give us wisdom.
- Colossians 4:2-4 – Prayer can open doors for the Gospel and clarify the message when it's communicated.

We have already referenced this last passage (Colossians 4:2-4), above. To expand the Kingdom of God, it is one of the most interesting passages of all. Prayer can unlock doors and hearts for the Gospel message. Just ponder that for a moment. If this is true (and, since it's there in the Bible in black and white, we have to believe it is), would we not want to pray for open doors far more often than we do? Would we not want to make a list of lost people – the "not yet believers" in our lives – and pray for open doors for each one of them?

This particular focus of prayer has been a tough one for me to comprehend. I understand God's power. But I also respect the free will that He has granted to all of us. So how does this prayer work? Although I don't have a clear answer, I know we have a clear promise. In Ephesians 1:11, Paul writes that God is at work, causing every little detail to come into conformity with His will. Wow. That's a powerful thought. Ultimately, He really is sovereign. To make sure I wasn't misunderstanding this verse, I went to the original language and checked every word, one at a time. The more I studied, the more confident I became in saying – God really is at work. The word here for "work" is sometimes best understood as a kind of decision. It takes into consideration His long-term plan. In fact, it almost describes a long-term **strategy**. It describes purposefulness. And it doesn't just involve believers only. The translation in the Message is justified. This verse can truly be understood as God, working out His purpose "in everything and everyone."

Now if that's the case, getting aligned with His purpose is

the only thing that makes sense. These are huge thoughts. They represent outlandish conclusions. For example, following this logic, think of just how closely prayer can be linked with outreach.

In the early 1980s, my wife and I were in Uruguay, trying to help launch a new church movement there in the city of Montevideo. We were walking through a shantytown populated by some of the poorest of the poor. We entered the shack of a man named Abel, who was an alcoholic. His wife, Carmen, was home from the hospital on what the doctors called a "dia de alto," a kind of "day off" that represented one of the last days she might ever spend with her little daughter, Marianela. Carmen had a bad case of double pneumonia and the doctors had all but given her up for dead. On that day, several of us gathered around Carmen and prayed like never before that she would be healed for the Glory of God.

Looking back, I'm not sure my faith was that great because I remember specifically asking God to heal her "within 30 days." God had other plans. He was already at work causing everything to come into conformity with His will. Two or three days later, we received a call from Abel, the alcoholic. He asked if he could give his testimony on the following Sunday in the new little church service we were trying to launch in that community. This was a rather radical idea. He rarely ever even **came** to the service. Why on earth would he be asking to speak?

As it turned out, Carmen had indeed returned to the hospital as planned on the evening of her "dia de alto." But on the following morning, when the doctors made their rounds and examined her, they were unable to find even a **trace** of infection in her lungs. Not a trace. Reluctant to jump to conclusions, they made some notes and determined to reexamine her the following morning. The next day, their exam revealed the exact same results. Carmen was completely healthy. Since hospitals are for sick people – and she was no longer sick – they released her without comment.

Abel was convinced that God had healed Carmen. His testimony will never be forgotten. They became the first fruits of that new little church service in the café, and that café service became our first church plant in the city. For me, it was a sign that God was with us in the establishment of His Kingdom for that zone of the city.

More Prayer: Our First Recourse

I never forgot those days. In fact, they have become a permanent part of my testimony as I retell that story again and again. It's a part of what anchors my faith and belief. God was at work, causing everything to come into conformity with His will.

When Jesus rescues us from darkness, He usually provides both redemption and lift, blessing us with an eternal home and a more hopeful home here on earth too.

Chapter 6
PUSH: PRAY UNTIL SOMETHING HAPPENS

In his little book, *PUSH: Pray Until Something Happens*, Jurgen Matthesius seeks to help readers discover God's dream for their lives so they can become the blessing they were meant to be for others. His conclusion? Take action, remain vigilant, and look for God at work at every step of the journey.

In the summer of 1991, my family and I were charged with leading a new Team Expansion initiative in Kherson, Ukraine, which was a part of the USSR. My wife was excited about the opportunity but sobered by the challenge. She had heard so many horror stories about the lack of medical supplies there – and the boys were young (ages 4 and 1). One day she confessed to me, "Doug, I just want to tell you now, I'll do my best to adapt to any and all circumstances. But if the boys become seriously ill, I'll be beside myself. Please promise me we won't ever have to rely on the medical system there. From what I'm learning, it seems to stem from an entirely different school of medical thought."

Of course, I told her everybody was praying and that it would all turn out ok. But, as it turned out, she didn't have to wait for long before there was trouble.

Back in those days, every flight into the USSR had to process through Moscow. Our flight ended up hitting bad weather. By the time we arrived, we had missed our connecting flight to Kherson. The airport where we had landed was rather rustic. We had taken along 5 Quest apprentices and 23 Pathways interns. (I know. It was kind of crazy.) I had a lot of plates spinning, trying to reconfigure flights for all these souls.

Suddenly, up walked my wife with our four-year-old in her arms. He was red as a firecracker – and completely listless. (If you were to have known our four-year-old at the time, you would have known he was **never** listless.) She had no idea what was wrong, but he definitely seemed seriously ill. (Yikes. We hadn't even completed our trip yet and the little guy was already sick!) I asked the group to stand by – and I said those words to Penny that I had prayed I wouldn't have to say: We'll have to seek out a medical opinion.

Of course, here we were in a strange (and rustic) airport. We didn't know a soul. We found a first aid lady. She indicated that our son should **immediately** be taken to a doctor. She mobilized an airport ambulance and, suddenly, it was Penny's worst nightmare. The doctor examined our son and concluded there was some kind of rapidly-developing infection in his blood. He insisted that our son be rushed to the largest pediatric hospital in Moscow. The ambulance transported us to the hospital running that famous European siren that they always play in those Jason Bourne movies. It was **not** a good day.

At the hospital, our greeting was a bit different from hospitals in the West. Even though things were rushed, I couldn't help but notice that the grass out front was nearly 12 inches high and the playground equipment had seen better days. In fact, I would have had to characterize it as old, rusty, and dreadfully unsafe – with jagged metal edges sticking out at multiple corners. I remember distinctly processing the thread in my head, "If this is the way they maintain the front yard, what's it like in the shadows?"

We walked in the front door, where we're accustomed to seeing some kind of lobby with an information desk and at least a plaque or two, if not an aquarium or a player piano. But in **this** hospital, there was no foyer at all. In fact, walking into the front door revealed a rather smallish room with four military cots. There were no sterile white blankets (warmed in an oven to help the child feel cozy). In fact, there were no blankets at all.

Taking note of the fact that we were foreigners though, someone brought an English-speaking doctor. In fact, it turned out that she was the director of the entire hospital. She wasted no time. (I remember thinking, "Don't we have to fill out a form first?") Within minutes, she turned to us and said, "Your son has an abscess. If we don't remove it, he could die any minute. We need to take him to surgery immediately. With that, a nurse started tightening a rubber hose around his little arm – and another attendant brought in a huge syringe that would have looked more at home in a veterinarian's office (maybe for a horse!).

I could tell Penny had just shut down. Honestly, I think she would have been more comfortable curling up into a fetal position in the corner. I stepped in the way and took off the rubber hose. (Penny looked at me as if to say, "What are you doing?") I remember trying to think of a joke in my head. I think I might try to resort to dumb jokes in times of high stress. As you can imagine, that habit doesn't go over that well with Penny.

I maybe said something like, "I don't suppose we could ask for a second opinion." I picked up our son, cradled him in my arms (by now he was barely conscious) and said, "I'm so sorry but I need a moment to think about this," and, with that, I thanked them and started out the door. That's when the Director spoke with a stern voice and retorted, "If you take your son out that door, he might die, and, if he does, his blood will be on your head." (Can you believe she said that out loud?) I continued out the door and Penny just followed as if in a dream.

I walked to the street, sat down on the curb and glanced back at the tall, gothic-looking building. Honestly, it looked like something out of a Batman movie during one of the dark scenes. Penny sat down beside me and said, "Now what do you propose we do?" There was an old, used syringe in the gutter of the street in front of us, looking very foreboding right there by our feet.

I answered, "I don't know. But we're not going to let that lady cut him open." Poor Chris. If he **was** still capable of hearing us, I can't imagine what must have been going through his little head.

At that point, I just prayed, "Lord, we need Your help. We've come all this way because we felt Your call to help these people learn about Jesus. But here we are, having not even arrived and, frankly, it feels like something – or someone – is trying to block our path. Would You please help us?"

At that very minute, a cab drove up and slowed down in front of us. This seemed to me to be somewhat of a small miracle already because we had heard it was next to impossible to flag down a cab in Moscow. I remembered the name of a tourist hotel in the city (from my language-learning tapes) and asked, in the best Russian I could manage, if he would take us there. He was happy to oblige.

In minutes, we were disembarking in front of what had to be the largest hotel in the city. Penny spoke urgently, as if everything depended on this next moment. "Doug, what are we doing here?"

Honestly, I didn't know how to answer her. It was one of those times in my life when I was just improvising. But we walked in the front door and, there, in the small lobby of this giant hotel was a brand-new aluminum telephone booth. Over the top of the door, in English, were the words, "International Calls." It looked out of place there, especially since we had heard that it was virtually impossible (at that time) to get a line out of the USSR to call **anywhere**.

We crowded into the phone booth. I was still holding our four-year-old in my arms. (It must have looked comical to others, the three of us crowding into that phone booth. But, at the time, nothing at all seemed comical to us.) I looked at the instructions and the only way a person could make an international call is by using an American Express card in the phone. It was crazy. I'm not kidding; I had taken out an AMEX card prior to departure, just in case we needed it while traveling. The card itself had just arrived **days** before we left.

Then Penny asked the really tough question, "Doug, who are we going to call?" I was still working on that. I had in mind to try to get in touch with our family doctor. But in doing the math in my head with the time zones, I figured it was probably Sunday morning back home in the USA. In fact, the math suggested it might be during our church service itself. So, I stuck in the card (and magically heard a dial tone) then dialed our local church in Florence, Kentucky.

Of all things, our associate minister answered. I asked quickly, "Dennis, is Doctor Caldwell there?" He said, "Well, I'm sorry, but he's in worship service and we shouldn't disturb him. Who is this, by the way?" I told him my name and he answered, "Well, I'm sorry, but I happen to **know** Doug Lucas and he's in the USSR, so, whoever this is, I'm going to hang up now."

I quickly shouted, "Dennis, I'm Doug Lucas and I'm calling you **from** the USSR – now please go get Dr. Caldwell!"

Dennis suddenly realized he was, in reality, talking to us in Moscow, and quickly scrambled to check whether or not Dr. Caldwell was there, in worship service. Within minutes, Dr.

26 | *Rescue From Darkness*

Caldwell was on the phone with us. We caught him up and he quickly sized up the situation.

"Well, it's sad because, it's probably not what we would do here, but you should probably go right back into the hospital, eat some crow, apologize for leaving, and ask her to operate."

I suddenly felt a **huge** lump in my throat. "Dr. Caldwell, they don't even wash bedsheets at that hospital. It's just not viable. And what do you mean, 'It's not what we would do'?" He went on to say something about not wanting to diagnose by phone and question another physician's opinion from a church service, 12,000 miles away.

I spoke more urgently. "Dr. Caldwell, please – let this be the **one** time in history that you diagnose by phone." His response was intriguing. "Well, I've heard that Russian medicine, in general, is much more likely to do exploratory surgery, whereas here in the West, we're more likely to try non-invasive alternatives first. This could indeed be an abscess, exactly as she's surmised, but these symptoms can also present in certain allergic reactions." This was so hopeful.

"So, if it were an allergic reaction, what might you try back in Florence, Kentucky?" There was now a strong dose of remorse in his voice. It was clear as a bell. "Well, you've told us there are no meds on the shelves there. So, it's all irrelevant. But if you were here, I might have tried a course of Benadryl first. I was so surprised.

"Dr. Caldwell, Benadryl sounds so tame compared to surgery. That would have been music to our ears, except – you're right. There's no way we'll ever find that here in Moscow in this epoch of shortages."

At that point, there, in that tiny phone booth, Penny started fumbling in her purse. The immediate thought that went through my mind was, "Here we are in a life-and-death situation, and she's apparently wanting to refresh her lipstick." But what happened next was too much for me to comprehend.

Out of her purse, Penny pulled a brown prescription bottle with a handwritten label that said, "Benadryl – in case you need it." It was signed, "Nancy." A nurse at a church in Northeastern Ohio had gathered some simple medicines to send with us for the kids. Penny said, "It all came in at the last minute. I just threw this in my purse."

PUSH: Pray Until Something Happens | 27

At that point, my eyes choked up with tears so much that I could no longer speak. I handed the phone to Penny and asked that she confirm that the dosage was right. It was. We started our son on that Benadryl and within hours, he was better. We were able to get everyone placed on flights to the South and within a very short time, were at work just as we had planned.

As time went on, we discovered a series of chigger bites on our son's legs and some were especially close to lymph nodes. Our pediatrician ended up concluding that one or more of those bites had become just infected enough to send that infection into the lymph node system. It rarely happens but when it does, it appears very serious, as we learned the hard way.

We still find it somewhat odd that the very illness that sought to undermine our arrival had likely started as our son played with other kids in some tall weeds on the campus of the Bible college where we staged the pre-field training for our team. Either way, we look back on this time as a true example of "God is with us." It's just too unlikely that the nurse in Ohio would have handed my wife a bottle of medicine – the very bottle of medicine we would need to move forward upon our arrival in this new land.

We give thanks to God for the fact that He is always at work in the lives of those who believe in Him. Maybe it was no accident that our son had this medical problem on Day 1 of this new venture. Remember, it was **the** very issue that Penny had indicated would be her undoing. Maybe some force wanted to attack us in the most sensitive area possible to cause the most damage possible. It was only a matter of days before we began to understand why.

Upon arrival in Kherson, we found an overwhelming sense of curiosity regarding all things Western. There was an intense fascination with **anything** that had been prohibited through the decades of iron-fisted communist rule. It didn't matter **what** we discussed: the people were open and interested in hearing it. So when we proposed the idea of showing the *Jesus Film* in the largest theater in town, all of our new friends were completely for it.

We were now trying to help a city of half a million people understand "who is Jesus," and they wanted to know. Communist authorities had permitted only one legal protestant church to serve the entire city. I had made friends with a young man from that church, a diesel mechanic named Zhenya. I asked him to go with me to the office of the director who would have to allow the film to be shown at the Jubilee Theater.

I remember sitting across from her desk as she gestured at the top shelf of her bookcase. My Russian was extremely basic, but she spoke slowly and clearly enough to understand every word. "You see here I have the entire works of Lenin on my shelf. There are 45 books and they symbolize 45 reasons why I can't let you show that movie in that theater."

It indeed seemed like a hopeless cause. She argued that the authorities would never permit it and the people would never allow it. I tried gently to persuade her. "But isn't it possible that the people won't allow us **not** to present it? And isn't it possible that showing the life of Jesus, the man who represents peace more than any other, would be the best medicine for this very moment in your nation's history?"

Nothing I said seemed to matter. She was very kind and yet she persisted, looking back up at those green books from Lenin, each with gold leaf trim that made them look almost sacred. I finally tried a different approach. Having heard that Soviet government leaders appreciate gifts of all kinds, I asked, "Ms. Director, isn't it a pity though that, although you have all the works of Lenin, it doesn't appear that you have the 66 books of the Bible. Wouldn't it make your library complete if you could also display the works of Jesus Himself?"

She leaned back and took a deep breath, introspectively. "But young man, I'm sure you must understand that such a thing would be quite difficult to obtain in our country. Where would you propose to find such a thing?"

I told her, "Ms. Director, I am a man of prayer. If I pray to find you such a thing and bring it back here for you, would you **then** consider renting us the theater? We would pay for its use and the funding could help you accomplish some of the goals you have for the arts in your fine city."

There was a long, pregnant pause. The diesel mechanic didn't move a muscle. Neither did I. She finally responded, "Mr. Lucas, if you can find such a thing, I would indeed reconsider your request."

We walked out of her office without saying a word. In fact, it wasn't until we had been sitting quietly in my little white

PUSH: Pray Until Something Happens | 29

station wagon for more than a minute when Zhenya finally spoke up, quietly, humbly, as was his custom. "Dooglahs," he said in his clear and simple Russian. Zhenya neither understood nor spoke English at the time. "What are you proposing to do now? Why are we sitting here in your car?"

I paused and then spoke, "We're waiting long enough to make it seem like it was challenging to find her a Bible." Zhenya looked perplexed. But in a moment, I gestured toward the back of the car. We got out and made our way to the back lift gate. There, inside my car, I had an entire **box** full of Bibles and, strangely, they were printed with green covers and gold leaf trim. I could never have pre-planned this.

Zhenya looked in the box then looked at me with a wry smile. "You knew all along that you had these Bibles here." We wrapped the Bible up in brown wrapping paper and tied it with brown string – like it was some kind of drug drop. We walked back into the office. When the assistant told us we could go on in, I touched Zhenya's arm at her door and spoke a quiet prayer before entering.

We walked into the office, thanked her for seeing us again, then placed the brown package on her desk. It was impossible to miss the excitement in her eyes. She carefully untied the string, opened the brown wrapping paper, then carefully and slowly cracked open the book, smelling of its freshly printed pages. She placed the book back in the brown wrapping paper as if she had just held a priceless archaeological artifact. Slowly, she raised her gaze toward us and asked, "So what dates were you needing the Jubilee Theater?"

The Jubilee Theater was packed out for 5 nights in a row. Audiences were enthralled. Over 600 people indicated a desire to follow up in home Bible study groups. By week's end, we had baptized a dozen people.

Prayer, along with that box of Bibles, became the lifeblood of that new work. I remember pulling into a gas station the night before I had to make the long drive to the Crimean Peninsula. I had to leave early the next morning but, sadly, every filling station had closed, reporting that there was no gasoline left in the city. This particular gas station was out by the airport and, sometimes, it was open a bit later than others. But tonight, it had closed along with all the rest. I was desperate, though, so I got out of my little white station wagon and walked up to the window of the control room. The curtains were closed, but there was a tiny light visible through the gap of the fabric. I pecked gently on the window.

A hand appeared, waving me away, and I heard a voice say, "There's no fuel. Go away."

I countered, "But I have to make a long journey tomorrow morning and this is my last chance to buy fuel." There was no response, only silence. I was desperate, and we wanted to distribute Bibles anyway. "What if I could get you a brand new Bible? Imagine! You would have your own copy of the words of Jesus."

The curtain slowly parted and a sleepy-eyed man appeared behind the glass. "You could do that?" I just nodded. The answer came back in a simple two-word sentence: "Pump One." After I refueled, I carefully wrapped a Bible up and walked around to the back of the station office. The door opened and we made "the drop." Honestly, once again, it felt like I was trading "arms for hostages" or doing some other illicit exchange. Except, in this case, I was exchanging the Words of Life in return for fuel to reach another town. I never forgot that man. "Pump One."

A week later, a coup took place in Moscow. A special "Emergency Committee" announced that they had placed Gorbachev under house arrest (just 3 hours from where we were living at the time). It threw the entire land into a tailspin. Helicopters were flying overhead, military equipment was in the streets, and politicians were giving speeches from atop army tanks in city squares.

That night, we invited 15 new believers to our house and, honestly, I could suddenly identify with Paul as he spoke to new church leaders in Miletus (Acts 20:17-38). I explained that no one could predict what was about to happen. I told them that some were saying that the Soviet Union would break up into civil war – and that foreigners could be expelled or arrested. One of the new believers was a ship's captain. He quickly interrupted, "Dooglahs, we can smuggle you out in a boat over the Black Sea." They were such precious people.

Either way, that night, I asked them how they would like to proceed. They asked, "What do people do in situations like this?" I explained that there was no playbook for this. But I told them that, if they were willing, they could form a new church and this group of 15 believers could be the initiative group that made it happen. They swallowed hard, but they each expressed complete willingness to participate in whatever way God called.

Looking back, that night **was** the beginning of the church in Kherson. They accepted the challenge. In the weeks that followed, we invested lots of time in Bible study, prayer, and leadership training. That foundation, born out of the calamity of their own nation's coup, brought them to the brink of fear and God's Spirit hoisted them over the wall from faith to fear. The Kherson Christian Church was real.

The days that followed brought additional challenges. Food was in short supply. People were scared for their very lives. One night, while staying up to listen to the Voice of America news, I looked outside the window and thought for sure I saw the image of a large bat on a branch of a tree. I even thought I heard it whispering my name. "Doug, go home! You don't belong here." I give thanks to God that He empowered me to respond, "In the Name of Jesus Christ, **you** are the one who should be gone." I never heard from that bat again.

As it turned out, Zhenya, the quiet diesel mechanic, ended up becoming the lead pastor of the church that God raised up. Twenty years later, when he invited me to speak at the anniversary service for the Kherson Christian Church, the fellowship had grown to be a church of nearly 1,000 people. They had started 65 daughter churches in nearby towns and villages and had sent missionaries to two foreign lands. When he introduced me, he told the story of praying outside the office of that theater director with the works of Lenin. He went on to say that he will never, ever again doubt the power of prayer. Neither will I.

Later in 1991, when the winter was well underway, having welcomed new workers to Kherson and with the new church work there well underway, we had relocated to the Crimean Peninsula where we were seeking to provide help and hope to refugees on the edge of the city of Simferopol, on the Crimean Peninsula.

It was already dusk by the time I approached a lady doing her laundry by hand outside the little shack that she and her husband called their home. With five inches of snow on the ground and no way to heat the water, I was saddened, but not surprised, to see just how blue her hands were from the cold. Like most of the Crimean Tatars in this village, however, she was an intrepid soul.

In my stuttering Russian (I was still learning Crimean Tatar), I asked for permission to approach her and explained that I was "a man of prayer, sent by a church on the mainland to pray for her people." I told her my name and asked if there was anyone around for whom I could pray on this early winter evening. She said her name was Gulia and she went on to explain that her husband had a terrible case of pneumonia and was inside her shack. She escorted me into the one-room house. Half the house was taken up by the bed. The other half was everything else.

She quickly made some tea, which I was glad to hold in my hands since it was the only source of warmth in the little village that night. I listened to their story. It was similar to the ones I had heard before. She and her husband were rustled up in the middle of the night on May 18, 1944, along with thousands of others. They were herded onto trains like cattle and whisked off to destinations like Samarkand in Central Asia.

The journey took some 22 days and nights, during which they were locked into railroad cars without so much of an explanation of why they were being deported. They lacked food and water and had no place to use the restroom. Records show that more than 200,000 of them were taken away in the dark of the night. Gulia became emotional as she described what sounded like to me was nothing short of a form of ethnic cleansing and human trafficking combined. Over 40,000 families were stolen away in just 3 days. Thousands died along the journey.

Once they reached Siberia and Central Asia, they were designated as "Special Settlers." This was a designation akin to calling them prisoners. It was a mass eviction. Soviet authorities and neighbors confiscated their 80,000 homes, furniture, and belongings. They were branded as traitors and despised by everyone. Some 20,000 soldiers took part in the armed operation. It was a dark time in their history.

They weren't permitted to speak their language aloud. Guards forced them to learn and speak exclusively Russian. They had one body of water to serve for every purpose – washing their clothes, cooking, watering their livestock, and even drinking. Crimean Tatars stored away all these memories. They will never forget. (Learn more at https://en.wikipedia.org/wiki/Deportation_of_the_Crimean_Tatars) That night, I prayed hard for Gulia's husband. It was well after dark by the time I said goodnight. I drove away from the village wondering how God would respond. I didn't have to wait long.

In the morning, I hadn't even gotten fully out of my little white Russian station wagon when Gulia came up and tapped on the window. "My husband's better," she said. "But can we please go pray for the little girl next door? She had pneumonia too."

They had her wrapped up so tightly in blankets, it seemed to me like a lost cause. Even if God healed her pneumonia, the odds of her survival were slim simply because she was wrapped so tightly, I doubted she could have gotten her breath anyway. But we prayed, just the same. Several neighbors gathered. I was just a bit nervous. This experience of praying for the sick wasn't new to me. But in this case, it felt like the locals were making it into a much bigger deal than I had ever seen previously. After praying for the neighbor girl, I decided to withdraw until some dust had settled. But this was not to be.

The next morning, Gulia met me again. "That neighbor girl is completely cured. The village chief, Jafir, wants to talk to you." I'm not sure why, but it felt a bit like I might get in trouble with the chief elder. After all, the entire village was Muslim. And my prayers had clearly been, "In Jesus' Name." Yikes. My mind quickly imagined all kinds of scenarios and frankly, none of them were all that positive. Still, I followed Gulia, who, by now, was muttering something about a widow lady.

Before I knew it, they were beckoning me into yet another shanty. There, in the middle of a slightly larger shack was Mumenye Apte, a 90-year-old widow lady bent over so far, it must have given her a sore neck just talking to the neighbors. They all explained that she was the oldest lady in the village and that she had no way to get warm. Using words I could only piece together by context, they explained how she used to gather firewood from the forest floor to bring back to her little salamander stove. The stove was cold on this morning, however. We could all see one another's breath clearly in her house as we visited. Soon, there was a quite a little crowd gathered.

Then came the moment when they introduced me to the

village chief. He was actually really nice. He explained that he would like to hear me pray for her. He couldn't figure out how prayers could be uttered at a location other than the mosque. This was all new to him. I gingerly approached Mumenye Apte and laid my hands on her shoulder and looked up at her sagging ceiling as if to peer out into the heavens. I opened my other palm in the way that I had seen Muslims pray. It was a longer prayer that day. I prayed specifically for coal for her stove. I asked God to bless all the neighbors and especially the village chief, Jafir. I prayed for Mumenye's back. It looked so uncomfortable. I gave thanks for the way that Gulia's husband and the girl next door seemed to be improving. And I thanked God for my new friends.

My family and I decided to invest the next day visiting coal yards. However, we felt like no one would listen. By the time we were done sloshing around in the snow, driving from one coal yard to the next, we had visited 16 different companies. No one would help. It was dark by the time we called it a day. I remember I started typing out my thoughts on our little laptop with a cracked screen. I wrote late into the night, wondering what tomorrow would bring. I didn't have to wait long.

The next morning, at least a dozen children met us at the edge of the settlement. I had brought my wife and sons with me to meet Mumenyeh. Gulia joined us as we walked those muddy, slushy paths to Mumenyeh's house. The little boys in the path kept trying to act something out for us – but I couldn't quite understand what they were saying. My Crimean Tatar was still so basic. But I kept hearing them make noise like the backup siren on a dump truck. When we rounded the corner, I finally realized why. There, in front of Mumenyeh's little shack, there was a pile of coal as high as the roof on her house.

The entire village was there. Jafir, the village chief, couldn't contain himself. He said there was enough coal to heat every shack in the village for the entire winter. Mumenyeh invited us in for tea. Her little salamander stove was as hot as a firecracker. Within a few minutes, I actually had to remove my coat because I was sweating. (She didn't remove hers.) It was a fun morning.

After thanking God for a coal yard supervisor with sympathy for the elderly, we enjoyed meeting other neighbors and, frankly, seeing some joy come to Dubki. As we walked toward the edge of the village, Jafir paused beside us and started musing about how he wished they had some gravel for their walking paths. I laughed. We didn't even understand how God had provided a mere bucket of coal, let alone a full dump truck!

But in the days and weeks that followed, there was more and more laughter. Jafir and his buddies would tell us stories long into the night. An enterprising Crimean Tatar businessman had opened a little kiosk on the corner, just down the path from Gulia's house. He and his family would insist every time he saw us that we should come in for more Turkish coffee. (Please don't ever tell him, but I was not a fan.)

Not long after God enabled us to find some gravel, the night finally happened. Jafir explained that the imam (the head Muslim religious leader for the entire peninsula) was coming to Dubki. Yikes. I swallowed hard. This could not be good. I remember the moment his little orange sedan rounded the path. He drove right up beside the house he wanted to use for the meeting. He was a tall man – with a body resembling Abe Lincoln's, I suppose. He climbed up on top of a partially constructed wall and began chanting the call to prayer like I had never heard it before.

Everyone came – the entire village. There was Gulia and her husband, the family with the little baby, and even Mumenyeh.

They all gathered in chairs placed in make-shift rows inside the large house on the corner. I think the Imam must have been speaking partially in Crimean Tatar, because I couldn't understand much of what he was saying. Jafir and I were sitting up front, near the place where he was speaking, but slightly to the side, so we were able to see nearly all of the crowd.

The imam read extensively from the Qur'an, but then raised his head and spoke to the people as if he was giving some kind of instruction. My curiosity was killing me. I finally leaned over to Jafir and asked what he was saying.

Jafir whispered, "He's telling us that you're no longer welcome in our village. He's forbidding us to speak to you again."

My skin grew hot. I looked only at the floor. I started assuming I would be deported just like Crimean Tatars had been deported. But, as I was looking downward, I heard a bit of a stir near the back of the room. I didn't raise my head. Suddenly, I heard the muttering of an elderly lady. It was Mumenyeh Apte. She had gotten up and was walking out of the room – which kind of shocked me, because the imam wasn't finished.

"What's that you're saying old woman," he asked. Then I realized – I was understanding them because she had spoken to him in Russian, rather than in her native language of Crimean Tatar. So he answered her in Russian. She continued, "When have you ever come to our village before? When have you visited our homes and tried to warm your hands by holding a glass of tea here? And have you ever prayed for even one of us to receive coal?"

He interrupted her rudely and retorted, "Old woman, I don't even know what you're talking about. I've never even **been** to your village before tonight."

"Exactly," she replied, as she spun around walked out. Another couple stood up next. As they turned, they said (again, in Russian), "And when have you prayed for our sick or for our elderly?" One by one, they all got up and walked out, until finally, by the end of a long awkward silence, the only people left in the entire room were Jaifr and I, along with the imam himself.

I didn't move an inch. I just kept looking down at the ground. The imam closed his Qur'an, folded up the little book holder he had brought with him, walked outside and, through the window, I could see him getting into his little orange car. Neither Jafir nor I spoke a single word – of any language. I just remember marveling that a man could be that tall and still fold himself up to fit into that little orange car. It was like watching a clown climb into a miniature car at a circus. After he drove off – and the night was still, I finally turned around and looked at Jafir and asked, quietly, "What does this mean? What do we do now?"

Jafir paused, then smiled and replied, "I guess we start praying for electricity."

In the weeks and months that followed, first there was one baptism, then two, then eight.

I actually returned in 2011 to speak at a 20-year anniversary celebration for one of the local churches God raised up while we were there. It was an amazing event. The church was averaging around 800 in attendance. They had their own staff, their own building, and had established some 65 churches in the towns and neighborhoods nearby.

PUSH: Pray Until Something Happens | 37

After the service, the Bible translator (who has since finished the entire Bible in Crimean Tatar) accompanied me to Dubki village. As we drove up, he cautioned me not to get my hopes up. "The village has changed a lot over the past 20 years, Doug, as you can imagine." When we got out of his car, he took off in one direction, trying to track down a volunteer who had helped him with translation. I set about trying to find something familiar – anything – among all the growth that had taken place. It was springtime and I approached a woman with her back to me, cutting tomatoes on the top of a large tree stump. I said, in my rusty Russian, "Excuse me ma'am? Would you have a moment?" She didn't even turn around.

At that moment, the translator came back around the corner as she spoke, with her back still toward me, "Dooglahs," she said. "Where have you been? My husband's sick again." She turned around to look me in the eye and added, "Would you be able to pray for him again?" The translator just shook his head and observed, "If I hadn't have just seen this with my own eyes, I would never have believed it." It was Gulia. She still remembered my voice after two decades. God rocks.

The last I heard, there were 30 baptisms and a strongly knit group of believers gathering weekly to celebrate, pray, and dream for the future. God can work a miracle any time He chooses. But for some reason, sometimes He waits to hear prayers from His people.

Everywhere we turn, we hear trainers emphasizing the importance of prayer as the fundamental catalyst to launch a movement. Jesus taught His disciples in Matthew 9:35-38 to "ask the Lord of the harvest" to raise up harvesters. If we want to multiply disciples and create a movement, we must learn to ask the Lord for that miracle. At the end of the day, multiplying disciples and groups is a spiritual battle, not a tactical one.

So, the instructions for spiritual battle in Ephesians 6:10-20 certainly apply to us.

"Finally, be strong in the Lord and in his mighty power. Put on the full armor of God, so that you can take your stand against the devil's schemes. For our struggle is not against flesh and blood, but against the rulers, against the authorities, against the powers of this dark world and against the spiritual forces of evil

in the heavenly realms. Therefore put on the full armor of God, so that when the day of evil comes, you may be able to stand your ground, and after you have done everything, to stand. Stand firm then, with the belt of truth buckled around your waist, with the breastplate of righteousness in place, and with your feet fitted with the readiness that comes from the gospel of peace. In addition to all this, take up the shield of faith, with which you can extinguish all the flaming arrows of the evil one. Take the helmet of salvation and the sword of the Spirit, which is the word of God. And pray in the Spirit on all occasions with all kinds of prayers and requests. With this in mind, be alert and always keep on praying for all the Lord's people. Pray also for me, that whenever I speak, words may be given me so that I will fearlessly make known the mystery of the gospel, for which I am an ambassador in chains. Pray that I may declare it fearlessly, as I should.

Garrison listed prayer as #1 in his Ten Universal Elements (page 33 of *Church-Planting Movements*). He emphasized that it was the vitality of prayer in the trainer's life that most predicted how engaged with prayer new pastors in the movement would be.

I heard from a friend that Ying Kai (known for catalyzing a huge multiplication movement in Asia) spent an hour every morning praying for God to work a miracle in his region. He told the same friend, "If one of the disciples I'm training comes to me explaining that he hasn't seen any fruit yet, I ask him to pull up his pant legs and show me his knees. If there aren't callouses there, I tell him I refuse to talk to him until he has callouses on his knees (from praying)."

During a training we staged in 2010, a relatively new team leader from North Africa attended. I still remember, during a break, when he came up to ask, "So you're telling me that one of the most important things I can do to launch a disciple-making movement among my nation is to raise up prayer?" We affirmed that yes, that was true. He looked back at us and asked, "So why haven't I heard this before?"

We realized, despite our best efforts, we still hadn't been emphasizing it strongly enough. (We have since redoubled and redoubled our efforts, again and again.) He went to work that year and, before we knew it, his team had set a goal of raising 1000 people to pray for his nation each day. After observing that it really wasn't THAT hard to recruit people to pray, he and the team decided to double the goal. When they hit 2000 people praying daily, they moved the goal to 10,000.

When they hit 100,000 people praying every day for their focus nation, something unique happened: A fruit vendor set himself on fire in a downtown square in protest of the nation's high taxes on roving vendors. Within a few short weeks, journalists were calling it the "Arab Spring." The next thing we knew, a revolution was shaking the country's government. The dictator went into exile in a foreign land. The new government immediately went to work crafting a new constitution and — guess what — the new constitution no longer made it a crime to convert away from Islam. In fact, residents were no longer asked at all about their religion on their national identity card applications.

Imagine if one of our workers had tried to suggest that that nation change its constitution, allowing more freedom for Christians in that land. We would have been laughed out of the country (or worse). But from everything we can observe, prayer did something that no politician could ever accomplish. And that team's work has continued to grow.

They had tried to open an evangelistic website, but it was futile. The government kept blocking their efforts. Lo and behold, the day of the revolution, the government's filter on the internet suddenly clicked off. By the next morning, thousands of local citizens had now exercised their new-found freedom to read Scripture portions and watch excerpts from the Jesus Film. Annual baptisms have climbed from zero to 14 to 40 to 72. Churches are starting to form. A new day has arrived. It all started with prayer.

Do you want to begin making a real difference? Do you want to spread the Gospel to the darkest regions? Start praying and don't stop. When we "PUSH – pray until something happens," it seems like something always happens. There are all kinds of ways to start a new mission work. To me, none of them are as fruitful and effective as prayer.

When Jesus rescues us from darkness, He sometimes transforms entire cultures, redeems whole villages, and works so mightily that it is impossible to doubt His presence. When that happens, there's no better place to be.

Chapter 7
MAKE YOUR CALLING SURE

I think A. W. Tozer might have been a genius. His writing is so clever. (When I grow up, I hope I can be 1/1000th as smart as he.) In his little piece, "On Breeding Spotted Mice," Tozer captures the essence of a wasted life. He tells the story of a "British peer" who had died just a few days short of his 89th birthday. "And what had he chosen to do," Tozer asks. "Well, according to the story, he had 'devoted his life to trying to breed the perfect spotted mouse.'"

Whenever I think of this story, I think of all the causes that occupy our time. I remember all the dreams we chase and I wonder, when we pass from this life to the next, which ones will matter.

I think Tozer was caught in the same set of questions. He wrote in this essay, "Made in the image of God, equipped with awesome powers of mind and soul, called to dream immortal dreams and to think the long thoughts of eternity, he chooses the breeding of a spotted mouse as his reason for existing. Invited to walk with God on earth and to dwell at last with the saints and angels in the world above; called to serve his generation by the will of God, to press with holy vigor toward the mark for the prize of the high calling of God in Christ Jesus, he dedicates his life to the spotted mouse – not just evenings or holidays, mind you, but his entire life."

When I think of such a man, I almost have to pity him. Surely there are moments in such an existence in which, even for a fleeting second, such a person wonders, "Why am I here? Where did I come from? Where am I going?"

Tozer finds just the right whimsical style to keep our attention and yet – to penetrate our hearts. He continues, "If the spiritual view of the world is the correct one, as Christianity boldly asserts that it is, then for every one of us **heaven is more important than earth and eternity more important than time.**"

That phrase just keeps rolling off my tongue. "Heaven is more important than earth" not only because it lasts so much longer, but also because of the higher stakes it entails. Tozer continues, "If Jesus Christ is who He claimed to be; if He is what the glorious company of the apostles and the noble army of martyrs declared that He is; if the faith which the holy church throughout all the world doth acknowledge is the true faith of God, then **no man has any right to dedicate his life to anything that can burn or rust or rot or die.**"

Yikes. When I read that sentence, I just want to go preach to some unreached people group somewhere. I want to live for a cause that lasts. I want my life to count. Tozer agreed. He went on to write, "No man has any right to give himself completely to anyone but Christ nor to anything but prayer."

And in the next sentences, Tozer actually set the tone for my entire take on "calling" and purposefulness. He writes, "The man who does not know where he is, is lost; the man who does not know why he was born is worse lost; the man who cannot find an object worthy of his true devotion is lost utterly; and by this description the human race is lost, and **it is a part of our lostness that we do not know how lost we are.**"

That, my friends, sums up the essence of unreached peoples. They are lost – and yet, part of their lostness is that they do not know just how lost they are. Tozer closes this paragraph with these penetrating thoughts: "So we use up the few precious years allotted to us breeding spotted mice. Not the kind that scurry and squeak, maybe; but viewed in the light of eternity, are not most of our little human activities almost as meaningless?"

So, it is upon finding our centeredness in Christ that we find purpose and meaning. Tozer put it this way: "One of the glories of the Christian gospel is its ability not only to deliver a man from sin but to orient him, to place him on a peak from which he can see yesterday and today in their relation to tomorrow. The truth cleanses his mind so that **he can recognize things that matter and see time and space and kings and cabbages in their true perspective.**" I just love that phrase. I wish so much I had written it. It's downright amazing. Tozer continues, "The Spirit-illuminated Christian cannot be cheated. He knows the values of things; **he will not bid on a rainbow nor make a down payment on a mirage**; he will not, in short, devote his life to spotted mice."

Each day we live, we should be asking ourselves, "Today, have I been bidding on a rainbow? Was my life invested in making a down payment on a mirage?" If so, then – what are we waiting for? Cry freedom today. Chase after a dream that rescues someone from darkness, not just for life – but for eternity.

Tozer closes his essay with this paragraph that I've never been able to forget. "Back of every wasted life is a bad philosophy, an erroneous conception of life's worth and purpose. **The man who believes that he was born to get all he can will spend his life trying to get it; and whatever he gets will be but a cage of spotted mice**. The man who believes he was created to enjoy fleshly pleasures will devote himself to pleasure seeking; and if by a combination of favorable circumstances he manages to get a lot of fun out of life, **his pleasures will all turn to ashes in his mouth at the last**."

I just keep imagining the man whose pleasures turn to ashes in his mouth. It's almost terrifying. I don't know about you, but I don't want to be that man. Tozer finished with these words: "He will find out too late that God made him too noble to be satisfied with those tawdry pleasures he had devoted his life to here under the sun." (You can read Tozer's original article, "On Breeding Spotted Mice," in his book, *Man – The Dwelling Place of God*, available on Amazon.)

In the preface to his little book, *Don't Waste Your Life,* John Piper writes, "The path of God-exalting joy will cost you your life [...] It is better to lose your life than to waste it. If you live gladly to make others glad in God, your life will be hard, your risks will be high, and your joy will be full [...] Some of you will die in the service of Christ. That will not be a tragedy. Treasuring life above Christ is a tragedy."

Lord, please help me grow up with those priorities: to treasure service over all things and to prioritize making others glad in God above trying to make myself happy. By risking it all for Christ's sake, I will truly find life. Jesus said, "Whoever loses his life for my sake will save it." Please count me in that number Lord Jesus.

Make Your Calling Sure

As far as my own calling, it seems all to stem from attending Qualifications at the Indianapolis Motor Speedway. That might not sound quite so spiritual – but for me, it ended up becoming that way.

My friend David had invited me for the day. His dad was a dentist, so their life felt upper class to me. They lived on a lake and had a boat and Ford Country Squire Station Wagon. So, it was a pretty big deal to get to travel with them from rural southern Indiana all the way up to Indy.

The morning started out as a beautiful, sunny spring day. We watched all the Indy 500 greats circling the track – Al and Bobby Unser, Mario Andretti, A.J. Foyt, and all the big names. There were so many people there. They have seating for more than a quarter of a million people, making it the highest-capacity sports venue in the world.

David and I decided to go down through the tunnel into the infield (the area inside the 2.5-mile loop). I'm pretty sure half of all those in attendance were inside of that loop. There were people of all sizes and all ages. We were so enthralled in watching those Indy cars come in for pit stops that we failed to notice that the sky had darkened.

Suddenly, a cloud-bursting rain started pouring down like cats and dogs. All 40,000 people squeezed into that tunnel at once. Somehow, I became separated from David. When we all burst out of the tunnel on the other side, the rain was coming down so hard, one could barely see. I glanced up in the grandstands. David's dad had already gone after the car. This was before the age of cell phones. I was lost and felt totally alone. I walked out into the parking lot and it was like a zoo. (Imagine 250,000 people trying to find their cars all at once.) I backed up against the wall of the grandstands, looked up into the skies, and started doing the only thing I knew to do: praying to God for help.

By now, I was completely water-soaked. Thousands of people were crisscrossing in front of me and I didn't know a soul. I asked God, "Lord, if You really are there, please send someone to help me." At that very moment, a giant white car began backing up toward my legs. I thought for sure I would be pinned against the back of the grandstand.

I looked up in the sky again and prayed harder. "Lord, I'll

do anything. I'll even go to Bible college if You want." As I looked up into the sky, searching for some sign from the heavens, I saw, directly above me, two mischievous-looking high school students who were dropping cans of beer on unsuspecting passersby. And right then, they dropped two toward **me**. The white car was backing up. The rain was coming down. I was about to be hit by two cold Budweisers – and so I prayed harder. "Lord, I'll even become a minister. I'll be anything You want me to be."

I'm not going to lie. At that very moment, I caught out of the corner of my eye a Country Squire station wagon stopping on my right. The back tailgate swung open and there was David Clark, beckoning me to come. I leaped over the bumper of the white car just about the time those two cans of beer hit the driver's trunk. Beer splashed up like a geyser. I ran to the station wagon and dove into the back.

David Clark asked me what just happened and I explained, "I think I just went into the ministry."

It sounds funny – but the most hilarious part of it all is – it's all true. The rest of my life I've basically just been keeping a promise. The reason I'm here today is because of the Indy 500, a cloud-bursting thunderstorm, and two Budweisers.

When I arrived at Bible college several years later, however, I experienced a bit of an inner conflict. It was really my first time away from home. Some of our classes were a bit more "open" than I had anticipated. They raised questions in my mind – doubts about the truth of the scriptures. It all seemed too heavy and complex. I began to doubt the trustworthiness of the Bible. I wondered about even the divinity of Christ and the existence of God Himself.

One particularly difficult morning, I walked out of chapel service and strolled up on a wooded hillside behind campus. I sat down on a log in a clearing and once again looked up into the sky. I spoke out loud. If anyone happened to be there that day, I'm sure they thought I was insane. But with real words, I said, "God, if You're really there, it sure seems hard to find You. But if You really **are** there, finding You would be the most important discovery of my life. If You would be so kind, please make Yourself discoverable and I pledge to search for You."

In the days that followed, I spent every free waking moment in the library, devouring books by leading apologists like Josh

Make Your Calling Sure | 45

McDowell, John Stott, C.S. Lewis, and others. I began collecting notes and typing something akin to a term paper. Some three weeks later, late in the dark of the night, I finished the paper and typed a title page, just as if I was going to turn it in to a professor. It was titled, "Why I Believe." I attached a blue slipcover to the paper and pushed my chair back from the desk.

There, in the dark, only illuminated by one solitary desk lamp, I realized I hadn't really proved God. But He had at least become a lot more believable to me than ever before. That night, I made a decision. I **decided** I was going to believe. I remember thinking that it wasn't a fireball from the wall. I didn't hear an audible voice. Instead, I made an intentional, intellectual decision. And again, for the rest of my life, I've just been depending on that one night's decision.

These experiences – like the Indy 500 and the night at my desk in the dark – they became like stakes in the ground for me. When I feel moments of doubt, I remember them and reiterate, "Doug, remember the Indy 500. Remember that term paper. Remember Carmen and her *dia de alto*," and suddenly, believing really does become a lot more believable.

And once one is sure of God, everything else falls into place. Remember what Tozer said? "The Spirit-illuminated Christian cannot be cheated. He knows the values of things; **he will not bid on a rainbow nor make a down payment on a mirage**; he will not, in short, devote his life to spotted mice."

I have not and I will not be cheated. I will not bid on rainbows. I will not make down payments on mirages. Instead, I'll give my entire life so that others can have access to a Good News story that prevents wasting our one life on a pair of spotted mice.

How will you live **your** life? How will make sure it counts? Remember, "The man who does not know where he is, is lost; the man who does not know why he was born is worse lost; the man who cannot find an object worthy of his true devotion is lost utterly; and by this description the human race is lost, and **it is a part of our lostness that we do not know how lost we are**."

Would you consider aligning your life with God's plan to redeem all of lost mankind and would you team up with us to help them find out about it? If you're willing, boy – do I ever have some opportunities for you.

When Jesus rescues us from darkness, He restores our souls and gives us a sense of purpose that makes us feel as if we are on a mission from God. The truth is, in fact, we are.

Chapter 8
RESILIENCE THROUGH SUFFERING

This past week, one of our newest Team Expansion missionaries came by for her Home Office Visit, having just wrapped up a one-year "Quest Apprenticeship" in West Africa. During her college years, she fought an extremely serious form of cancer not once but twice. A young woman with a lesser faith might have wavered. But not **this** young woman. She kept her focus on God and prayer. Cancer left her with incredible challenges to overcome. One by one, she has overcome them all.

As we talked, the conversation turned to the value of prayer through suffering. She admits that there were times when things grew dark. But now, one can't possibly miss the inner joy in her life. In fact, while we were discussing the challenges life throws our way, she reminded me that it helps to have a sense of humor. Robert Kohls writes about this in his little book, *Survival Kit for Overseas Living* (Available on Amazon). In fact, he holds that a sense of humor turns out to be the most critical factor for effective cross-cultural adaptation. Being able to laugh at one's self – and be laughed at by others – turns out to be the most helpful agent for cross-cultural effectiveness **and** fruitfulness.

Paul writes in 2 Corinthians 1 that the encouragement or "comfort" we receive when we go through the most severe trial will, in the end, help us give encouragement or comfort to others (2 Cor. 1:5-7). Multiplying our abilities can have a supreme impact, both for us and for the Kingdom.

Venezuela has proven to be one of Team Expansion's most fruitful fields. Entire megachurches have come about through the power of the Lord working through our team members there. But during the start-up, there was a time when things looked pretty bleak. An annoyed neighbor was complaining like crazy about all the racket we made while singing on a Sunday morning. It was, in fact, touch and go as to whether we would be able to stay in the large building we had rented.

I remember the night that the team and I sat down to make a final decision as to whether we should stay. We prayed long into the dark of the night. All of us were getting pretty sleepy, so I finally suggested to the group that we ought just to draw straws – literally. I walked into the kitchen area and found a box of soda straws. I grabbed a dozen out of the box and used some scissors to snip a couple of inches off of the end of one of the straws. Mixing them together, I held them up in front of me with my hands covering up the ends. Not even I knew which of the dozen straws was the shortest.

I walked out back onto the balcony where we were praying. Thousands of lights twinkled up on the hillsides surrounding Caracas. It was a beautiful sight, and we were sure that God was with us among all those lights. But we had to make a final decision. I held the straws up to our youngest worker and asked him to choose a straw. I remember him looking around at the dozen or so faces of his teammates, asking, "So, if I pick the shortest straw, we stay no matter what?"

The group all agreed. "No matter what, come what may." He instantly reached out and without hesitating drew one of the straws and, sure enough – it was the one I had snipped.

I can't say whether God would advise us to put out a "fleece" in all situations, but I can tell you that, that night, it was good enough for me. I smiled at the group and without saying a word, headed upstairs to hit the sack. I figured God had spoken. After brushing my teeth, I happened to think that maybe the group needed to debrief that moment a bit more. I came back down the stairs and there they were, all seated silently, nobody saying a word. They hadn't moved an inch.

It's a sobering thought to consider that one might just have heard the voice of the Lord speak into a sparkling starlit night.

That team went on to become one of our best, serving side by side for more than 20 years. The complaining neighbors actually were one of the first families to come to Christ. Once they began taking part in the singing, they never complained again. The police forgot all about the complaint because the neighborhood became the most peaceful place in town. Hundreds and hundreds of Venezuelans have come to Christ and we now have Venezuelan missionaries serving side by side on multiple teams all over the world.

God spoke. The team listened. It always works better that way.

When Jesus rescues us from darkness, He sometimes speaks in a way that gives assurance that He'll be with us always. Even in the midst of a chaotic world, there's no better place to be than by His side.

Chapter 9
YOUR MISSION, IF YOU DECIDE TO ACCEPT IT

I enrolled in Bible college not really having any clue what I would do. As I began my second year of study though, I was sure of one thing: Surely, I didn't need to take the course they were about to require. It was called "Introduction to Missions." Honestly, I really didn't have any idea what "missions" was! My home church had said almost nothing about it. I had never heard of a mission trip. And the thought of going overseas was about as likely for me as making a trip to Mars.

So, I scheduled an appointment with the president of the college to ask for an exception. I told him, with deep respect, "This seems like a huge waste of money. I'll never use **anything** that I learn in that class."

The president lowered his glasses on his nose and asked, ever-so-formally, "Mr. Lucas, if I'm not mistaken, do I recall that you're here on a scholarship?"

I replied quietly, "I am, sir."

He responded, "And do I recall that it's called 'The President's Scholarship?'"

"It is, sir."

I was starting to see where he was going with this line of questioning. I felt as if I was on a witness stand in a murder trial. "And do I recall that it's a 100%, all-expenses-paid scholarship?"

"It is, sir."

"So, if we'd like to pay you for taking this class, and if we fail to see it as a waste of money, is it really costing you anything Mr. Lucas?"

"Well sir, ..." (I fumbled through the catalog.) "I see that it's a 2-hour course sir. But I see here that there's a 3-hour course called, 'Principles and Methods of Missions.' Since it actually entails more study, might I substitute that class instead?"

He paused. "So you're willing to work 50% harder for that class? Might I ask why?"

"Well of course, sir. You see, the catalog says that it begins with 9 weeks of Bible study. It's not that I want to get out of work. I just want the work to matter – with deep respect sir. And Bible study is **always** a good thing, right sir? So, with deep respect, at least I'll be receiving **some** kind of redeeming quality out of the class – even if I'm never going to serve for a day in anything remotely related to missions."

His smile almost seemed whimsical, almost as if he were participating in a party trick. "I'll grant that exception, Mr. Lucas."

And so it was that I began 9 weeks of Bible study in "Principles and Methods of Missions." Throughout the next 2 months, day by day, we worked our way through dozens of scripture passages, most of which are listed below. I'm not going to lie; I just had never considered these passages seriously before. Nearly every single class was like a new light bulb going off in my head. And following every class, I'd emerge with some new thought, challenging all my assumptions and priorities. (See the addendum at the end of this book for some of those Scriptures and the ways the Holy Spirit convicted me as we studied them.)

By the time we hit mid-terms, 9 weeks later, I nearly came to class with my bags packed. I was hooked. And it wasn't a fireball coming out of the wall. It wasn't an audible voice from God. It was pure, crystal-clear scripture. The **Bible** called me to missions.

After those first 9 weeks, I went back down to the president's office and informed him that I wished to change my major to missions. He smiled that same wry smile, nodded his head, and simply said, "That's good." Before I graduated, I ended up taking every missions course the college offered, including the original Intro class that I had tried to dodge. I've been working in missions ever since.

A few years back, I was helping with a new field survey in Tanzania, West Africa. We were interviewing local people in a village far down south, almost to the border with Mozambique. At the time, 9 months out of the year, all the roads would wash out in the rainy season. The only way in was by bush plane, landing on a small grass landing strip.

We scattered into various villages and I ended up interviewing a Makua man named John, sitting at a campfire with his four wives. After 30 minutes of interchange about subjects as varied as the weather to the way he planted his crops, I finally asked, "And what about the man named Jesus. Have you ever heard of him?"

John paused for a moment, then adjusted his gaze from the fire up into my eyes and responded, "Does he live in Mtwara, out by the sea?"

I answered slowly, "Well no, it's a little more difficult to explain. He doesn't exactly live just in one place. He lives inside of me – and inside the hearts of all those who pledge to follow him."

John answered, "I need to know about this man." My Makua was non-existent. My Swahili wasn't much better. But I pledged to send someone back to tell him about "this man Jesus."

Once I was back in the USA, I sent him a letter. I wasn't even sure it would ever find him. After all, his campfire was as isolated as the grass landing strip where our plane landed. In that letter, I gave him my word that we wouldn't forget his village. We wouldn't forget his tribe. We wouldn't forget his name.

Recently, one of our workers on that team visited our International Services office in Louisville. Our worker explained to me that, recently, John's compound caught on fire. The fire eventually spread to John's own hut. At great risk to life and limb, John ran back into his burning house to retrieve his most prized possession: that letter I had sent him. Why? Because when our workers arrived, John found them and showed them the letter. Our workers fixed a date to travel out to John's mother's village. As they rounded the last turn in the old dirt road, our workers couldn't believe their eyes. There were hundreds of Makua tribespeople waiting for our workers. They wanted to hear about this man who lived in their hearts.

Today, there are many Makua churches and many Makua leaders. Among them, there's a man named John who now knows that Jesus isn't a man who lives in Mtwara out by the sea. He lives much closer than that. He now lives inside of John's heart.

When Jesus rescues us from darkness, He passes to us the capacity to rescue many others and to train those others to reach still others.

Your Mission, If You Decide to Accept It

Chapter 10
A STRATEGY FOR LAUNCHING DISCIPLE-MAKING MOVEMENTS (DMMS)

A disciple is a follower of Christ who hears, obeys, and shares the Good News with others, and then trains others to do the same. Put another way, a disciple loves God, loves people, and makes disciples. So how does a disciple become a disciple maker? How can disciple makers participate in rescuing others from darkness?

Today, we are in the midst of what just might be the greatest awakening since the first century. In David Garrison's 2004 book, *Church Planting Movements,* the author shares cases in which many people, sometimes hundreds of thousands of nonbelievers, are coming in droves to embrace faith in Christ. Furthermore, many of these new believers are immediately going to work sharing their testimonies, often in the face of severe persecution. Garrison refers to these experiences as **church-planting movements, defining them as "a rapid multiplication of indigenous churches planting churches that sweeps through a people group or population segment"** (page 7).

On pages 33-36, Garrison sums up his findings by sharing ten **"Universal Elements"** that he finds in many of these movements.
1. Prayer
2. Abundant gospel sowing
3. Intentional church planting
4. Scriptural authority
5. Local leadership
6. Lay leadership
7. Cell or house churches (Cell churches are organized meetings arranged by the leadership core of the movement, while house churches are more dynamic and

not necessarily arranged by a central leadership core.)
8. Churches planting churches
9. Rapid reproduction
10. Healthy churches

On pages 37-40, he goes on to share ten **"Common Elements,"** which were nearly as widespread and equally instructional.
1. Worship in the heart language.
2. Evangelism has communal implications, growing along family or social connections.
3. Rapid incorporation of new converts into the life and ministry of the church.
4. Passion and fearlessness.
5. A price to pay to become a Christian.
6. Perceived leadership crisis or spiritual vacuum in society.
7. On-the-job training for church leadership.
8. Leadership authority decentralized and leaders can act interdependently, without having to seek permission from a higher authority.
9. Low profile of outsiders by drawing new believers into leadership roles through participative Bible studies and mentoring them into the role of pastor from behind the scenes.
10. Suffering of missionaries.

These elements (both universals and common) framed a backdrop for additional movements that still others began to notice worldwide. These movements have been called by various names, including the following:
- **CPM:** Church-planting movement
- **CMM:** Church multiplication movement
- **SCMM:** Sustainable church multiplication movement
- **T4T:** Training for trainers
- **DMM**: Disciple-making movement

The coalition of mission organizations known as "24:14" has refined and expanded on Garrison's findings. Taking their name from Matthew 24:14, they have described the terms, Church

A Strategy for Launching DMMs | 55

Planting Movement (CPM) and Disciple Making Movement (DMM), as approaches that emphasize the following characteristics:
1. Spirit-led
2. Every follower is a multiplier
3. Peer accountability
4. Become a disciple worth multiplying
5. Here, near, and far-vision
6. Multiplying disciples, churches, leaders, and movements
7. Emphasizing **biblical** principles of multiplication

What kind of life should we live to reduce barriers and allow God to work such a miracle in front of our eyes? In other words, what are the daily habits, the life practices, and the **strategies** that seem most likely to produce a disciple-making movement? Having watched, studied, and carefully observed the formation of these movements, we humbly suggest that the following seven habits seem most effective and fruitful in clearing the way for God to do such a miracle. We propose that **all serious followers of Christ** should begin immediately seeking to live out these seven life practices to the fullest amount possible.

NOTE | As you explore these habits, many tools and resources are available to you at zume.training at no cost. At the Zume site, we've provided instructional videos, courses, further study, and tools for application.

Pray

Jesus taught and modeled much about prayer. His followers caught the bug. It seems that everything that happened in the book of Acts came about as a result of prayer. In a very real way, the entire story begins in Acts 1:14 when "... All these with one accord were devoting themselves to prayer..."

When Jesus saw lost people, He was always moved deeply and He often prayed for them. For example, in Matthew 9:35-38, when Jesus saw that people were harassed and helpless, "like sheep without a shepherd," He told his followers to "ask the Lord of the harvest" to raise up harvesters. We too, must learn to ask the Lord for that miracle. At the end of the day, multiplying disciples and groups is a spiritual battle, not a tactical one. So it should come as no surprise that all of the instructions for spiritual battle apply fully.

As a result, we recommend that would-be disciple-makers, as well as churches that want to multiply, begin with fervent, over-the-top prayer. Begin by analyzing how much you pray for the lost, personally. Ask your church leaders to help you keep track of how much your church is praying for lost people. The answers might be shocking. When examining themselves and their churches, some have found that we are praying for the lost for only a handful of minutes each week, if that.

Throughout any strategy for Kingdom advancement, every single step should be bathed in prayer. Some great DMM trainers have, for example, encouraged that we pray at least one hour every day. Some of the practices and strategies below will **sound** as if they are up to us. Nothing really is. It's all up to God. We can't say it enough. Pray, pray, and pray. Only God can bring about a disciple-making movement. Ask Him to do so.

Recommended Action Steps:
1. Decide to pray more for lost people.
2. Make a list of 100 people who are not yet believers. Pray for them daily.
3. Pray. More.

Obey

In 1988, Nike, the shoe company, pioneered a giant media campaign centering on 3 simple words: "Just do it." The first commercial featured an 80-year-old man named Walt Stack. "People ask me how I keep my teeth from chattering in the wintertime," he quipped as he jogged along the walkway of the bridge, cars whizzing by. The emphasis on action was unmistakable. Today, more than ever before, we need disciple-makers who will "just do it" – obey, rather than merely hear.

We would never be so foolish as to think that walking into a garage transformed us into a car. How did we ever imagine that **merely** walking into a church would transform us into a follower of Christ?

How can we help followers of Jesus today to embrace a

A Strategy for Launching DMMs

culture of simple obedience and action? James wrote, "Do not merely listen to the word, and so deceive yourselves. **Do what it says** (1:22)." In fact, Jesus didn't tell His apostles to make disciples of all nations and **"teach them"** everything He had commanded. He told his followers to "teach them **to obey** (Matthew 28:19-20)." In John 14:15, Jesus said, "If you love Me, you will keep My commandments."

We can worship equally well in a crowd of 5000 as we can in a crowd of 5. But mentoring, modeling, and measuring obedience is next to impossible unless we can walk alongside those we're seeking to influence. Think about it: We can transfer content in a classroom. But we have no idea what people will **do** about it. Accountability sounds, at first, like a terrifying word. But it's not so scary if it happens naturally, as a part of a community of followers who are living, modeling, walking, and constantly talking with one another. Accountability, and the action that it prompts, is exactly what we need today – more than anything else.

Recommended Action Steps:
1. Decide right now that you will be a person of action and obedience.
2. Start today by sharing this message with someone else.
3. Begin seeking God in everything. Ask him to fill you up.

Share

One missionary/evangelist put it this way: "The growth of any movement is in direct proportion to its success in mobilizing its total membership in the constant propagation of its beliefs" (International Bulletin of Missionary Research, 1979).

If we want to help God's Kingdom advance, we have to talk about it. Christ's followers understood this concept. In Acts 4:20, Peter and John concluded that there was no way they could keep quiet about what they had seen and heard. In Mark 5:19, Jesus told a brand-new follower to start out by telling his "own people" how much the Lord had done for him and how He had had compassion on him.

This idea of telling one's own people, sometimes described by trainers as one's "oikos" (the Greek word for "household") is so solid. It's a tremendous place to start because it can open up an entirely new sphere of interest for the Good News. And make no mistake: This new follower had known Jesus for less than a day. Jesus didn't require a long class on doctrine. He put this new follower to work instantly.

What can we share if we've just met Jesus for the first time? We can tell the story of how He is changing us. That's "My Story." And in time, as we learn the story of God's redemptive acts throughout history, we can also tell God's story. Trainers have provided templates for these two kinds of sharing. These templates can help us learn to transmit the entire Gospel – the story of Jesus and His life, death, and resurrection – and how it has changed us.

Certain biblical passages, like Ephesians 4:11-12, suggest that some believers have a gift of evangelism. Let's seek them out and count on them to be especially fruitful in sharing their faith. But other biblical passages make it clear that, one way or another, we **all** have to sort this out and engage.

In Matthew 28:19-20, Jesus made it clear to the disciples that He wanted them to teach every new baptized believer how to obey his commands – and the command that would have still been ringing in their ears was the very command to make disciples of all nations. So it was incumbent on the disciples to "pass on" all the training they had received, including the training to share faith with others in hopes that the whole world would embrace Him. Signing up to become a believer is signing up to become an ambassador for His Kingdom (2 Corinthians 5:18-20). Ambassadors, above all else, **represent**!

Remember early on when we encouraged prayer? This is another one of those occasions. Prior to every instance in which we share the Good News, let's ask God to speak through us. We might be the one voicing the words, but let's ask **GOD** to empower us and speak through us. Let's ask Him to lead us to the people He would like us to reach. Let's place our total dependence on His power.

Recommended Action Steps:
1. Learn and practice how to tell "your story."
2. Learn and practice telling the "3 Circles Life Conversation."
3. Get started sharing your faith by prayer-walking in

friendly neighborhoods where people are out and about. Pray to God for boldness to share your story and His story. Every time you practice, you'll feel more confident. Keep doing it – and you'll get better at it.

Train

In Acts 16:3, we learn that Paul wanted to take Timothy "along on the journey" as they multiplied disciples and groups. Just as Jesus had trained His closest followers, the disciples now wanted to train others. Paul later told Timothy, "And the things you have heard me say in the presence of many witnesses entrust to reliable people who will also be qualified to teach others."

Trainers often have compared these concepts to a flock of ducks, walking through a meadow. At the front of the line, a mother duck knows and leads the way. The duckling behind her follows along dutifully. Each duckling in the line has a responsibility to follow in the footsteps of the duckling ahead, while also setting the pace for a brother or sister behind.

This metaphor is perfect for summarizing Paul's instruction to Timothy. It's also perfect for understanding our responsibility as followers of Christ today. We not only follow the example of Jesus, but in addition, we lead others to do the same. And we don't have to know the entire journey when we take the first step. We just have to be one step ahead of the duckling behind us. We don't have to know **everything** before we can start training others on **something.**

Remember our encouragement to pray? This is another one of those times that we depend largely on God to be at work within us. If we try to do all of this training on our own, depending on our own devices, we will most certainly fail. Let's ask Him to empower us and speak through us. Ask Him for wisdom regarding the people we consider training. Then, as we train them, let's pray that He will be at work in all and through all.

Recommended Action Steps:
1. Internalize the idea that God can use you to help the duckling behind you, even as you keep learning from the duckling in front.
2. Invest time in learning God's word, but then share it with

others.
3. Learn and practice how to baptize someone so you'll be ready. Train others.

Gather

In the early church, believers gathered constantly (Acts 2:44). There were few locations for large crowds, so most of their meetings were in homes. (See, for example, Acts 12:12.) In the context of small groups, we find true accountability – something that is much more difficult in large weekend celebrations. Therefore, movements often encourage both kinds of meetings – large-scale celebrations for worship and training, alongside smaller home-based groups for discussion and accountability. Because those groups are so numerous, however, it's difficult to recruit and prepare experienced teachers for each home group. As a result, movements needed a different model. Enter the Discovery-based Bible study.

Discovery-Based Learning as the Motor
Interestingly, even though these movements have arisen on different continents through the hands of a wide spectrum of trainers, most have at least this one factor in common: They all end up having to rely on discovery-based learning rather than lecture-format teaching.

When reading and studying a Bible passage, discovery-based learning focuses on a set of questions, usually something along the lines of:
1. What did you like about this passage?
2. What did you find difficult about this passage? (What didn't you understand?)
3. What does this passage teach you about people?
4. What does this passage teach you about God/Jesus?
5. How will you obey this passage?
6. Who will you train with this message?
7. With whom will you share your story or the story of God?

These seven questions (or questions very similar to them) make up the pivotal core of what many CPM/DMM trainers call a Discovery Bible Study or DBS. Because this study incorporates a bit more than a Bible study and because it's so different from a classical Bible study as we know it, in this book, we prefer using the term, "3-thirds group" to help learners understand that this is not your typical Bible study. A 3-thirds group is a gathering of 4-12 people who want to learn to love God, love others, and make disciples.

Now you might be asking, "How can a bunch of questions elicit any kind of content that's worth hearing?" This group interaction with the passage, inspired directly by the Holy Spirit, brings out so many insights. It also elevates the Word and gives the Bible the highest regard because, instead of focusing on an outline developed by a preacher, the group is focusing totally on the outline in Scripture.

But there's another benefit. Because there is no real "leader" exactly (only a group **facilitator**), everyone feels positioned as an equal. What this means is that it no longer matters if one of the group members has a degree from a seminary, while another member has just opened the Bible for the first time ever. The Bible is the revealed word of God. It's powerful enough to speak on its own. At the same time, this helps lay the groundwork for group members turning into group starters. It also helps newcomers feel welcome to participate.

Furthermore, by participating, we engage more with the passage than we would if we were merely hearing about it. What's more, even the absolute first-timer brings a fresh perspective and can find hope in the Scripture. Beyond all this, our common sense tells us that the more we can stay engaged with learning, the more interesting learning will be.

There might be another reason why discovery-based learning is working so well in these movements. We all enjoy discovering something on our own. The seven questions asked in a discovery Bible study help us apply what we learn, connecting ideas with actions. We stay engaged, our mind has to focus, and we find it easier to tell someone else about what we studied.

Now we know it's easy to scoff at this and say, "This isn't biblical." Right. Cultures vary profoundly, so how can one learning approach have ever become so popular in a particular style of group multiplication? Right. All those criticisms and many more could be leveled. Here's an equally profound conclusion: Hundreds of thousands (maybe millions?) of new believers have demonstrated the ability to learn this simple approach (discovery-based Scripture learning) and then rapidly replicate it among others. In many cases, they've shared it rapidly with non-believers. Our conclusion, after examining scores of these case studies, is that God seems to be using this approach in our day to grow His church and expand His Kingdom in **wildly** effective examples.

Indeed, discovery-based learning isn't the **only** way to study the Bible; but we heartily recommend that learners try it, if for no other reason than to understand why it has been working so effectively throughout the rest of the world.

Peer Accountability
Many of us have been involved with Bible studies down through the years. We've participated in life groups, adult Bible fellowships, Sunday School, and many other small gatherings. We might have even visited something similar to a discovery Bible study. So why are THESE discovery Bible studies producing such incredible growth? One of the major reasons is the action orientation spurred on by peer accountability. At the close of the discovery Bible study, we ask three critical questions:
- How will you obey this passage?
- Whom will you train with this message?
- With whom will you share your story or the story of God?

This idea of keeping knowledge, application, and teaching all at an even rate of development can be seen in passages like 2 Timothy 2:2. "And the things you have heard me say in the presence of many witnesses entrust to reliable people who will also be qualified to teach others." We see it in the parable of the talents (Matthew 25:14-30). We see it in Matthew 10 where it says, "freely you have received freely give." We see it in Luke 12:48 where it says "from those to whom much has been given much shall be required." We have to trust the Holy Spirit in believers and His Word along with being responsible in our application of accountability within the body to be enough.

Recommended Action Steps:
1. To foster spiritual growth in our lives, we all need

A Strategy for Launching DMMs

accountability.
2. Sort out how your life will work in a pattern. It helps. You could view it as taking part in three time slots each week – a home church for worship and celebration, a small group (like a 3-thirds group for your friends/believers) to help you stay accountable, and also a regular time slot for outreach – like regular weekly prayer-walking or maybe a different 3-thirds group for unbelievers.
3. Now that you understand the big picture, why not facilitate a Zume Group for your friends and fellow-believers? Learn more here at the course page: <u>zume.training</u>

In a typical Bible study that is focused on content/knowledge, some participants hide under the radar. In one of these groups, with peer accountability, it's pretty impossible to hide out. So what happens to the people who don't really want to obey/implement? They typically self-select out of the group after a few weeks. Furthermore, maybe they should. In a CPM/DMM approach, we want to encourage members who are willing and able to implement. Peer accountability acts as a kind of filter to find and encourage those people.

Our Assignment is Faithfulness; Let God Worry About Fruit
As we attempt to gather, we have to remember that many (most?) of our groups will fail. It's just the nature of this work. People move away. They grow weary. They become disinterested. Satan snatches them from our grasp. For these and other reasons, as we gather, we have to remember to pray constantly for those we are attempting to reach. Only God can bring about a disciple-making movement.

Suggested Action Steps:
1. Start a 3-thirds group this week.
2. Soon after starting your first group, help someone else start a group.
3. Understand your role as a facilitator and not a lecturer.

Multiply
The entire book of Acts is about the expansion of the early church.

In Acts 6:7, Luke records that the Word of God was spreading so quickly, it was no longer resulting in "additions" to faith. At that point, it had started to multiply.

For growth to happen through multiplication, every single person has to catch fire in his or her everyday living. This sense of personal responsibility is key. What's more, each believer has to figure out how to pass on faith in such a way that the person with whom they are sharing can **also** pass it on. And beyond all this, God has to be at work. (Did we mention before the importance of praying in and through all of this?)

Today, more than ever, we need disciples and groups that multiply like rabbits, not elephants – and certainly not mules. You see, mules are born sterile. They can't reproduce because they are hybrids. Elephants can reproduce, but they sure take their time in doing so. The typical elephant requires 18 to 22 months to have a baby elephant and when she does so, she only has one calf. Imagine, even if you can get the cooperation of the elephants, in 4 years, you'll likely only have (at maximum) two new calves.

By contrast, **rabbits are absolutely wild**. In the first place, the typical pregnancy for a rabbit lasts roughly one month. One. Month. What's more, a litter of bunnies typically consists of at least five new baby rabbits – but there **can** be as many as a dozen! And get this – the mother rabbit only requires 24 hours to recover from giving birth before she can become pregnant again. So once again, if you can get the cooperation of the rabbits (and it sounds like you will), and if zero rabbits die (we did the math on this), after just 48 months (4 years), you'll have a grand total of **53 septillion bunnies**. That's a lot of rabbits. That's 53 X 10^{24} or 53 with 24 zeroes after it. That's well over 7 times the population of the entire world. In just 4 years. Wow. Let's multiply.

Reproducibility

Because we are constantly seeking to multiply, we have to figure out how to do everything in reproducible ways. For example, if we meet with others to train them on prayer or accountability, we should avoid meeting in restaurants and buying their meals/coffees every time. Why? Because our goal is not only to train others, but to model the **process** of training others. What if some of our group members feel they can't afford buying meals or refreshments every

A Strategy for Launching DMMs

time? If that's the case, we can't possibly stage our 3-thirds group in a rented facility. Everything we do has to be reproducible. We design the entire system to multiply from the beginning.

At the End of the Day
Because movements come only from God, none of this is up to us. We can't say it enough times: We could do all of these things perfectly well and **still**, a movement might never happen because only **God** can make a movement. For this reason, even when we focus fully on multiplication, we have to focus fully on prayer.

Recommended Action Steps:
1. Make the mental shift to begin to view yourself as a multiplier.
2. To multiply more effectively, you'll need to search for a "person of peace."
3. As you multiply, keep track of the growth using a chart to help you with coaching.

Grow

Throughout the whole book of Acts, the emphasis was on growth—spiritually, organically, and numerically. The day we have become complacent about growth is the day we start dying. In some ways, the goal is to snatch as many people from the fire as quickly as possible (Jude 1:23), then once everyone has heard, relax our pace just a bit to focus on "perfecting the saints" (Ephesians 4:12).

For a child to learn to ride a bicycle, he needs to be able to get on the bicycle and will probably fall a few times before he has enough expertise to be able to ride proficiently. There is no way around this. People need to get on the bicycle and be allowed to fall before they learn to ride well.

We must become more accepting and more forgiving of mistakes, especially early on in a disciple's development. When someone comes to faith and immediately starts trying to apply and share, he or she might indeed make mistakes. But, again, that's like children learning to ride bicycles. That's natural and normal. We don't chide children for their efforts. We applaud their efforts and help them to do better. We continue to aid and supervise as they continue to grow and improve until they get to the point at which they can ride the bicycle on their own.

    We tend to use knowledge as a measure of maturity when there is no such thing. Maturity takes time, and there is no way a new believer can be totally mature in his faith. We spend too much time focusing on maturity. Instead, we should focus on faithfulness. I believe faithfulness can be measured best by the ratio of how much someone knows, to how much they obey, apply, and pass on what they have learned to others.

Epilogue

For the last 45 years, while leading a missionary-sending organization, various friends and peers have asked, "How did you do it? How did you get up every Monday morning and go back at it for another week?" But the truth is, honestly, it has never even felt like I was going to work. It doesn't feel like a job. The only thing I can answer is that when a person's passions are aligned with their actions, there is such an agreement of "will" and "obedience" that service happens out of compassion rather than compulsion.

Every month, each Team Expansion worker meets with his or her supervisor for an employee review. I'm no exception. I meet each month with the Chairman of the Leadership Task Force (Team Expansion's board of directors). In our meeting earlier this week, Todd and I were brainstorming about "the missionary call." At one point, he reflected, "You know, we weren't necessarily called to an easy path. We were called to put one foot in front of another in Godly obedience." That was a helpful observation. Your favorite Team Expansion missionary would probably openly admit to you that some days are easier than others. But none of us signed up for these roles because they were easy. Rather, we signed up because we knew the Cause was worth it.

At the end of the day, how do we define, "calling," anyway? Our conclusion is that it's simple obedience to God's command. If you can see the need and if you have decided in your heart that you could be a part of meeting that need, you, my friend, are already called.

I've got this friend named Shawn. The more I get to know him, the more I understand the way God can rescue someone from darkness. Shawn's story speaks to me. It inspires me.

He grew up in a single-parent home, raised by his mother. He shared, "My parents divorced by the time I was 6 or 7 years old. Both were alcoholics. Looking back, I can see how my mother was dealing with past traumas from her marriage, and possibly childhood too, and the pain of it led her to drink herself to death. My father did as well. My mom struggled with raising me right with no dad in the picture. The truth is, I was abused a lot when I was young. But little did I know at the time, I had a Father in Heaven who had His hands on my life. My mom struggled with fears and anxiety too, and when she wasn't drinking, she wasn't happy and got angry a lot. She passed those things on to me as well, and for all of my life, I had trouble with them, which kept me from expressing myself."

One of the striking conclusions I draw when hearing a story like Shawn's is that we often don't cause our own darkness. It often descends on us from another source. I wonder what life would have been like for me if I had faced the challenges Shawn faced. He told me he moved out of his home when he was just 15. He ended up staying with one of his mom's ex-boyfriends. "Within the first month," he remembered, "I was introduced to heroin. I struggled with heroin, off and on, for the next 20 years when I wasn't in jail or prison. It was a vicious cycle for me. If I wasn't in jail, I was either using or selling drugs, and even visiting Mexico to get them. I was 18 the first time I ended up in prison. It was a three-year sentence. I think it was there that I first prayed to God, having believed that Jesus died for my sins and was raised from the dead. I asked Him to save me."

Shortly after that first three-year sentence, Shawn, now in his early twenties, made one of his trips to Mexico, this time solo. He remembers, "I decided to have a few drinks the night before I returned back to Houston, Texas. That night was the beginning of the realization of the power of prayer in my life, and how God saved me from dying that night. Laying on my back on one of the side streets, with rope burns around my neck, and the white of my eyes red from bleeding out, I was listening to the two men standing over me, talking to each other. Eyes closed, and not even wanting to breathe, I was as good as dead and the last thing I remember after telling God I was sorry and asking Him to help me was waking up hog-tied to a fence in a field in the middle of nowhere in my socks and boxers. It shows the grace our Father has for us, in His long-suffering and love. It's also a good reminder for me that I may never forget that He saved a wretched sinner like me."

One of the attributes I appreciate most about Shawn is his ability to be self-aware of both his own struggles as well as the mighty power of God trying to work within him. He told me, "From the age of 15 to 33, I was either in prison or in the streets getting high, trying to numb myself from a past with chains I couldn't escape. But there's no pit God's grace cannot pull us out of, and there are no chains that Jesus can't break off of you. During those years, through my intravenous drug use, I ended up carrying the Hep C virus for some time too. On my last visit to prison, I was 27 years old. I was living in hell, and to be honest, I was relieved in a weird way when I was arrested, knowing I wouldn't be able to continue that vicious cycle of waking up sick and looking for that next temporary fix. Going to court, as I pleaded guilty to my charge through the arrest process, the district attorney offered me a 45-year sentence on my first court appearance. I'd still be in prison today if it hadn't been for God intervening. My public defender sat down with me and explained that something had happened to the district attorney. In his place, the court had assigned a substitute D.A. who just happened to be his college buddy. His buddy offered a 10-year take-it or leave-it deal. I thank God for being my Judge that day in court. And to top it all off, after receiving a bit of favor due to some community college courses I took, I ended up being released after serving just 6 years and 3 months. I ended up in Oregon."

Looking into Shawn's life is like looking into a snow globe while the snow is still falling. This is all so recent. As I write these words, he was just released from prison three years ago. All of his memories are still so fresh. He remembers those six years in prison because they only just happened recently. "Those 6 years were a real turning point for me," he reflected. "The first week I was there, I picked up a Bible and started to read through Genesis, because I didn't know how else I could show Him I cared about Him. I was truly hoping to find answers to help me. But I'll be honest: none of it made sense to me at the time. I began praying and praying and praying that God would hear me – and help me. In some ways, God had already saved my life, but I felt remorseful because I hadn't changed directions, acknowledged Him, or even sought a relationship with Him. I learned that we truly don't know what God's grace is until we experience it in ways that cannot be explained. I began little by little to understand His great mercy, unmerited favor, and undeserved Love. But I also began realizing that it is impossible to stop God's plans for His purposes in our lives, sometimes even after rejecting His Love."

Shawn's journey to know Jesus was rocky. He remembers his mother taking him to church some when he was 8 years old. He shared with me, "I have a vague memory of a Sunday school class in which I was taught how to talk to God in prayer. I have thanked God many times for the fact that He led my mom to take me to church then. From those few experiences, at least I had an idea of God, and I knew that I could talk to Him. The truth is, I didn't really do much praying. It was more like a conversation with Him, along with praying for others. After I was in Oregon for about a year, I found myself in a place where I was broken. I didn't want to be alive anymore. I wouldn't have killed myself, but I wanted to be dead. My dad killed himself through alcohol and drugs, and my mom too, and it was as if I had been trying to follow their lead my whole life with my lifestyle and drugs. Although I wasn't using heroin anymore, I didn't go a day without smoking cannabis. One night in the bathroom, I was telling God how sorry I was. I thought of everything I had done in my life. I remember apologizing to him even for all the things I couldn't remember. I asked Him for forgiveness and to give me a purpose and a reason to live. That was the night. That prayer changed my life."

So, like many of the other instances of "rescues from darkness," Shawn's unique experience with Christ began with prayer. In fact, that specific night was a turning point for him. "I don't remember if it was that night, or a couple of nights later," he tried to recall, "but laying in my bed, I experienced the Holy Spirit come on me. It was as if it washed me in a way that could literally be felt. He filled my heart with an indescribable love beyond anything I have ever known. Everything began to change for me after that night. Slowly, I began my journey with Him. It was as if the Holy Spirit had to love me back together first, before He plowed my heart, and churned the soil, so that His seed could grow. There was a fire in the process for me, too – a purifying process, a sanctification process – that came in stages for me. It was as if God was slowly pulling the weeds out of my heart and mind. Throughout the last two years, Jesus has removed the guilt and shame from my past. He's taken away bad habits, along with the anger, fears, and depression from my life. All those sins had been keeping me in bondage. I now experience a peace in my heart that never goes away, and a love and joy that only He can give. He's healed me in so many ways. I've had three tests done now in the past three years for Hep C. The doctors are amazed that the virus is no longer detected in me. I owe everything to Jesus, and have dedicated my life to Him in every possible way that I can. I'm all in – wherever and whatever He leads me to do."

Some time later, Shawn ended up here in Louisville. For the first year here in Kentucky, Shawn still used cannabis regularly — until one day he had another encounter with Christ. The memory of that day is seared into his consciousness. "I had been working on laying some flooring and painting walls in an empty condo. During a break, I was lying on my back again and I was thinking about going to get some cannabis after the day ended. While my eyes were shut, I had a kind of vision of someone standing in front of a brilliant white light. I could see the silhouette of His body with His arms stretched out hovering in the distance as I was looking at Him in a sea of blackness behind my eyelids. I had promised Him I would quit, and as I was looking at this, I knew it was Jesus. He touched His chest where the lungs are and said, 'You promised me. You promised me.'

"God speaks to us today. He speaks mostly to us in His Word. God speaks through messages in sermons to us too, and through other Christians. But in this case, it was as if He was speaking directly to me. It wasn't an audible voice that I could hear, but a still small voice. I don't know how else to explain it. The silhouette of His body disappeared and then there was a brilliant white light of a silhouette of His face shining with an outline of thorns around His head, to show me it was really Jesus, and it was as if His face was right in front of mine. Suddenly, He smiled. There weren't details in His face, but enough to get a glimpse of His smile where dimples would be."

Shawn is all in. He doesn't shy away from a challenge. The night before he was supposed to be baptized, his car broke down. He was so afraid he would miss church (and his baptism) that he decided to take off on foot — the night before. His baptism was slated for a church building that was 13 miles from the place where he was staying. He remembers the walk, and the temperatures, so well. "I didn't dress warm enough and should've had a coat on that night. The temperature dropped and the wind picked up. It was freezing and all I had was a t-shirt. I was cold, to say the least, and would find shelter every hour from the wind as I marched down the streets. About half way there I prayed, asking God to give me a sign that He was still with me. I couldn't understand why my vehicle had broken down the night before, and I wasn't in good shape. No more than 3 minutes later, as I was walking around 3:00 am, there, in the middle of the road was a clear, see-through plastic "roll bag," with a glow stick that was broken in it. I could see that the lime green/yellow light stick was shining, and it was sitting inside the bag with a brand-new blanket. I'm not making this up. There aren't any words I can say that could express the way I felt in that moment. All I could do was cry, knowing that somehow, someway, He answered with more than that sign, but also gave me comfort from the cold that night."

In many ways, Shawn is like the consummate example of a "rescue-from-darkness" story. This is exactly why we get up in the morning – to find people like Shawn who will experience transformational changes like he has. And he understands that, now, it's also his honor and responsibility to help pass along that transformational story to others. He shoots straight with it. "May my testimony strengthen the faith of others, and show others how God is always with us. Even when we don't think He is there, He is always there. May my testimony show others how important prayer is, and that He hears our prayers, and is always listening, and answering them, and not always in the way we expect. And sometimes it's a no. And even then, it doesn't mean He isn't there with us through our ups and downs. He always has a way of working all things out for the good of those who love Him. And most importantly, may my testimony show others how important it is for us to make sure that kids know who Jesus is. Had my mom never taken me to church, I would never have known. I would never have tried to have a relationship with Jesus."

May God multiply Shawn's story many times over tomorrow, and the next day, and in the years to come.

So please, my friend, please don't waste your life. In fact, don't waste another moment. May God bless you in the fulfillment of His calling to you for the expansion of His global Kingdom.

When Jesus rescues us from darkness, He makes life worth living and takes away all fear. Join us on that journey. You'll never regret it.

Addendum

MISSIONAL SCRIPTURES

To give proper credit where credit is due, everything I learned about the below Bible passages and themes came from my missions professor, Tom Gemeinhart. When I heard that he had passed away from this life, I made the trip back to Grayson, Kentucky, to attend his funeral. In fact, his wife and family even asked me to speak, saying that "Professor Gemeinhart considered Team Expansion to be one of the greatest fruits that had ever come out of his teaching." But to me, the greatest fruit that ever came out of his teaching was the pure and simple truth that we'd better get busy because a lot of people need to be rescued from darkness.

All emphasis added is mine.

Old Testament

Genesis 12:1-3
The Lord had said to Abram, "Leave your country, your people and your father's household and go to the land I will show you. I will make you into a great nation and I will bless you; I will make your name great, and you will be a blessing. I will bless those who bless you, and whoever curses you I will curse; and **all peoples on earth will be blessed through you.**"

    Notice that the promise was that **all** peoples on earth would be blessed – not just all "people." The definite message here is – every tribe.

Genesis 49:10
The scepter will not depart from Judah, nor the ruler's staff from between His feet, until He comes to whom it belongs and the obedience of the nations is His.

> The one who should inherit the scepter and staff would be Jesus. God had in mind for every nation to obey Him.

Exodus 19:3-6
Then Moses went up to God, and the Lord called to him from the mountain and said, "This is what you are to say to the house of Jacob and what you are to tell the people of Israel: You yourselves have seen what I did to Egypt, and how I carried you on eagles' wings and brought you to myself. Now if you obey me fully and keep my covenant, then out of all nations you will be my treasured possession. Although the whole earth is mine, you will be for me a kingdom of priests and a holy nation. These are the words you are to speak to the Israelites."

> Israel was supposed to be an entire "kingdom of priests." What do priests do? They serve as a go-between, between God and man. So, it seems that Israel was supposed to do the same – to act as a go-between, enabling all others to see God through them.

Numbers 14:21
But as I live and as the Glory of God fills the whole Earth—not a single person of those who saw my Glory, saw the miracle signs I did in Egypt and the wilderness, and who have tested me over and over and over again, turning a deaf ear to me—not one of them will set eyes on the land I so solemnly promised to their ancestors.

> Notice that the Glory of God was designed and determined to fill the **whole** earth, not just part of it.

Deuteronomy 32:43
Rejoice, O nations, with His people, for He will avenge the blood of His servants; He will take vengeance on His enemies and make atonement for His land and people.

> Whenever we see the word, "nations," in the Bible, it typically means "Gentiles," i.e., "not Jews." The essence of this verse is that even Gentile nations have something to celebrate. This

verse means that Jews **and** Gentiles were both to be blessed!

I Kings 8:43b
…then hear from heaven, Your dwelling place, and do whatever the foreigner asks of You, so that all the peoples of the earth may know Your name and fear You, as do Your own people Israel, and may know that this house I have built bears Your Name.

This is Solomon, uttering a special prayer at the dedication of the temple. Can you imagine how strange it must have been for the Jewish people to hear their king asking God to answer the prayers of non-Jews? What a concept?! Yet that's exactly what Solomon prayed would happen. Every time we (non-Jews) pray today, we experience a bit of an echo (a fulfillment) of this prayer. God intended even "not Jews" to approach His throne along with Jews.

Psalm 18:49
Therefore I will praise you among the nations, O LORD; I will sing praises to your name.

Remember, when you see the word, "nations," think Gentiles. This Psalm predicts praising alongside the not-Jews!

Psalm 24:1
The earth is the LORD's, and everything in it, the world, and all who live in it;

The clear message here is that everyone on earth was supposed to follow God.

Psalm 67
May God be gracious to us and bless us and make His face shine upon us, that Your ways may be known on earth, Your salvation among all nations. May the peoples praise You, O God; may all the peoples praise You. May the nations be glad and sing for joy, for You rule the peoples justly and guide the nations of the earth. (Selah) May the peoples praise You, O God; may all the peoples praise You. Then the land will yield its harvest, and God, our God, will bless us. God will bless us, and all the ends of the earth will fear Him.

This prayer is clear and simple: The psalmist is praying that God's salvation would come to all nations. Everything we do today in missions seeks to bring about the fulfillment of this same prayer. "May **all** the peoples praise you." Once that happens, only then will we see the earth truly yielding its intended harvest. Only then will we experience the true blessing of God.

Psalm 68:32
Sing to God, O kingdoms of the earth, sing praise to the Lord,
The message is simple: all kingdoms on earth (not just the Jews) were intended to sing praises to the Lord.

Isaiah 52:10, 13-15
The Lord will lay bare His holy arm in the sight of all the nations, and all the ends of the earth will see the salvation of our God. [...] See, my servant will act wisely; He will be raised and lifted up and highly exalted. Just as there were many who were appalled at Him – His appearance was so disfigured beyond that of any man and his form marred beyond human likeness – so will He sprinkle many nations, and kings will shut their mouths because of Him. For what they were not told, they will see, and what they have not heard, they will understand.
Most commentators see this as a clear prophecy of Jesus. Either way, the import here is clear: **all the ends of the earth** will see the salvation of God. And He will "sprinkle many nations," meaning that He will show His mercy to all of them.

Isaiah 54:3
For you will spread abroad to the right and to the left, and your descendants will possess the peoples and will people the desolate cities.
These "desolate cities" could only be describing non-Jewish cities. There are still many desolate cities today, waiting for the Good News. They are "hidden" from that Good News today, sadly. Let's do something about that. No valley is too isolated. No island is too distant. No forest is too dense. No mountain is too inaccessible. No city is too fortified. No desert is too hostile.

Isaiah 60:3
Nations will come to your light, and kings to the brightness of your dawn.

These other nations, led by other kings are all Gentile – not Jewish – kings. This verse describes us today!

Isaiah 62:2
The nations will see your righteousness, and all kings your glory; you will be called by a new name that the mouth of the Lord will bestow.

Many commentators believe that this verse is a prophecy of the new name of "Christian." Either way, here's that word, "nations," again.

Ezekiel 18:4
For every living soul belongs to Me, the father as well as the son – both alike belong to Me. The soul who sins is the one who will die.

Every. Living. Soul. Not just Jews.

Ezekiel 33:6
But if the watchman sees the sword coming and does not blow the trumpet to warn the people and the sword comes and takes the life of one of them, that man will be taken away because of his sin, but I will hold the watchman accountable for his blood.

The Lord told Ezekiel this story for a purpose: If He gave the people a message and they listened, they would be saved. But if they didn't listen, then they were the guilty ones. But here's the thing: If the watchman fails to deliver the message, then it isn't the **people** who are guilty. It's the watchman himself – for withholding the important news. We have been given a message to share. We dare not keep silent. If we do, their blood will be on our heads.

Jonah – The whole book.

Remember, Jonah didn't want to go to Nineveh. But he learned the hard way – one can't run away from God. He was a "reluctant missionary." And what might be the people group to whom God sent him??? It was a Gentile city! No wonder he didn't want to go! This is a picture of future "centrifugal" outreach. The situation demanded proclamation. Jonah was apparently an effective presenter; he just didn't want to go. May we not be guilty of repeating his sin.

Micah 4:1-2
In the last days the mountain of the LORD 's temple will be established as chief among the mountains; it will be raised above the hills, and peoples will stream to it. Many nations will come and say, "Come, let us go up to the mountain of the LORD, to the house of the God of Jacob. He will teach us his ways, so that we may walk in his paths."

The law will go out from Zion, the word of the LORD from Jerusalem." Again, the emphasis is on "many nations." We'd better get busy.

Zechariah 2:10-11
"Shout and be glad, O Daughter of Zion. For I am coming, and I will live among you," declares the LORD. "Many nations will be joined with the LORD in that day and will become my people. I will live among you and you will know that the LORD Almighty has sent me to you."

Again – many nations.

Malachi 1:11
"My name will be great among the nations, from the rising to the setting of the sun. In every place incense and pure offerings will be brought to my name, because my name will be great among the nations," says the LORD Almighty.

There it is again – "the nations."

New Testament

The missionary message of the New Testament became more centrifugal (as was foreshadowed by the book of Jonah). Eventually, the whole church got involved. There were several key themes. Among them:

- The Christian God is the only true God (1 Corinthians

8:4, Acts 4:26, Acts 4:12)
- The Christian God is concerned about all people (John 3:16)
- All men are sinners (Romans 3:23, Romans 5:12, Romans 3:9-12)
- Man's nature is corrupted (Colossians 1:22-23, Eph. 2:15)
- Those who continue in sin are lost eternally (Ephesians 2:12)
- Salvation is found only in God's son (Luke 19:10, Acts 4:12)
- To have salvation, we must respond in faith (Hebrews 11:6, Romans 10:9-10, John 20:31)

Matthew 8:11

I say to you that many will come from the east and the west, and will take their places at the feast with Abraham, Isaac and Jacob in the kingdom of heaven.

Now the message is getting clearer: God **never** intended this to be a message solely for Jews.

Matthew 9:35-38

Jesus went through all the towns and villages, teaching in their synagogues, preaching the good news of the kingdom and healing every disease and sickness. When he saw the crowds, he had compassion on them, because they were harassed and helpless, like sheep without a shepherd. Then he said to his disciples, 'The harvest is plentiful but the workers are few. Ask the Lord of the harvest, therefore, to send out workers into his harvest field.

> The harvest belongs to Him. We're supposed to ask Him to raise up workers to go share among those who haven't yet heard the Good News. How many times has your church prayed this prayer? Here it is, a clear command in the New Testament.

Matthew 24:14

And this gospel of the kingdom will be preached in the whole world as a testimony to all nations, and then the end will come.

> Here it is – finally – loud and clear. God's will is that all nations should hear the testimony of His Word and His

will. Once that happens, time will end. Are you yearning for heaven? Would you like to see Jesus return? Then finish the task.

Matthew 28:19-20
Therefore go and make disciples of all nations, baptizing them in the name of the Father and of the Son and of the Holy Spirit, and teaching them to obey everything I have commanded you. And surely I am with you always, to the very end of the age.

When I heard these words, everything fell into place. He wants us to go – to travel to all nations, sharing the Good News, baptizing them, and training them to do the same with others. Multiplication has always been the plan – all the way until the end. Why in the world did we ever think "church" consists of going to a meeting and hearing a message and then not doing anything about it? These were some of the last words Jesus spoke on this planet in bodily form. When people share "last words," they aren't just talking about foolish things. We take a person's "last words" very seriously. Can you see why these scriptures impacted me so much?

The following scripture should all be very clear now. See what you think.

Mark 16:15
He said to them, "Go into all the world and preach the good news to **all creation**.*"*

Luke 2:10
But the angel said to them, "Do not be afraid. I bring you good news of great joy that will be for **all the people**.*"*

Luke 10:2
He told them, "The harvest is plentiful, but the workers are few. Ask the Lord of the harvest, therefore, to send out workers into his harvest field."

Luke 24:47-48
…and repentance and forgiveness of sins will be preached in his

name **to all nations**, beginning at Jerusalem. You are witnesses of these things.

John 10:16
I have other sheep that are **not of this sheep pen**. I must bring them also. They too will listen to My voice, and there shall be one flock and one shepherd.

John 12:32
But I, when I am lifted up from the earth, will draw **all men** to myself.

John 20:21
Again Jesus said, "Peace be with you! As the Father has sent me, **I am sending you.**"

Acts 1:8
But you will receive power when the Holy Spirit comes on you; and you will be my witnesses in Jerusalem, and in all Judea and Samaria, and **to the ends of the earth.**

Acts 4:12
Salvation is found in no one else, for there is **no other name under heaven given to men by which we must be saved.**

Romans 1:16
I am not ashamed of the gospel, because it is the power of God for the salvation of **everyone who believes**: first for the Jew, **then for the Gentile.**

Romans 10:14
How, then, can they call on the one they have not believed in? And how can they believe in the one of whom they have not heard? And **how can they hear without someone preaching to them?**

II Corinthians 5:20
We are therefore **Christ's ambassadors**, as though God were making his appeal through us. We implore you on Christ's behalf: Be reconciled to God.

Ephesians 2:12
Remember that at that time you were separate from Christ, excluded from citizenship in Israel and foreigners to the covenants of the promise, without hope and without God in the world.

This verse in particular just haunts me. I wake up in the middle of the night sometimes just thinking about it. People who are outside the covenant of the Jews – and outside the New Covenant – have no hope **because** they are without God in the world. May it not be. May we help them face the world **with God** as their Lord.

II Thessalonians 1:6-9
God is just: He will pay back trouble to those who trouble you and give relief to you who are troubled, and to us as well. This will happen when the Lord Jesus is revealed from heaven in blazing fire with his powerful angels. He will punish those who do not know God and do not obey the gospel of our Lord Jesus.

I'm haunted by this verse too. It's talking, in particular, about Hell. And who are the people who will be punished? Those who "do not know God," right alongside those who have chosen not to obey Him. Let's speak forthrightly: I don't **like** this verse. It doesn't seem **fair**. But I didn't **write** it. And I don't get to make the rules. It's God's universe. Only He can make the rules. So I don't want to wait around and count on some kind of special dispensation of mercy (even though I might **hope** for such a thing). For the time being, I have to **assume**, based on this verse, that those who don't **know** God can't possibly call on Him to be saved. So they are **lost**. That is tragic. Now that you know this, what are you willing to **do** about it?

I Timothy 2:3-6
*This is good, and pleases God our Savior, who **wants all men to be saved** and to come to a knowledge of the truth. For there is one God and one mediator between God and men, the man Christ Jesus, who gave himself as a ransom for all men – the testimony given in its proper time.*

III John 5-12
Dear friend, you are faithful in what you are doing for the brothers, even though they are strangers to you. They have told the church about your love. You will do well to send them on their way in a manner worthy of God. It was for the sake of the Name that they went out, receiving no help from the pagans. We ought therefore to show hospitality to such men so that we may work together for the truth. I wrote to the church, but Diotrephes, who loves to be first, will have nothing to do with us. So if I come, I will call attention to what he is doing, gossiping maliciously about us. Not satisfied with that, he refuses to welcome the brothers. He also stops those who want to do so and puts them out of the church. Dear friend, do not imitate what is evil but what is good. Anyone who does what is good is from God. Anyone who does what is evil has not seen God. Demetrius is well spoken of by everyone – and even by the truth itself. We also speak well of him, and you know that our testimony is true.

> We infer from this that John (the apostle) had written a reference letter for Gaius. It was intended to pave the way for Gaius and his team to speak at various churches and among various preaching points. But there was a man by the name of Diotrephes who blocked the path of Gaius and his team. John said Gaius was good because he was "on a journey for God's name." But Diotrephes was bad because he wouldn't help Gaius on his way. We become like Gaius (a fellow helper of the truth) whenever we help a person on a journey for His name's sake (a missionary). The Greek word for "show hospitality" ("propempo") can be translated as "provide food," or "provide housing," or "provide money," or "go with" a person." When we "propempo" a missionary, it's like we are a fellow helper like Gaius. No wonder that churches down through the centuries have prioritized missions so highly. May we not stop.

Revelation 5:9-10
And they sang a new song: "You are worthy to take the scroll and to open its seals, because you were slain, and with your blood you purchased men for God from **every tribe and language and people and nation***. You have made them to be a kingdom and priests to*

serve our God, and they will reign on the earth."

Revelation 7:9-10
*After this I looked and there before me was a great multitude that no one could count, from **every nation, tribe, people and language**, standing before the throne and in front of the Lamb. They were wearing white robes and were holding palm branches in their hands. And they cried out in a loud voice: "Salvation belongs to our God, who sits on the throne, and to the Lamb."*

More From the Author

AS A FOLLOWER OF JESUS, WHAT'S THE ONE THING YOU CAN TAKE WITH YOU FROM THIS LIFE TO THE NEXT?
The answer: More Disciples. More Disciples is a practical, how-to guidebook that lays out a clear path for learning and implementing church-planting movement (CPM) and disciple-making movement (DMM) strategies and life principles. It includes, in text form, all of the concepts of the web-driven course, ZumeProject.com.

Author Jerry Trousdale said, "More Disciples is truly an excellent resource for people wanting to get started, or get better at, catalyzing multiplying disciples. But it will also be a very useful reference resource for CPM/DMM veterans."

The truth is, this book could change your life — as well as the lives of your neighbors and nation. Read it, then most importantly, do it.

THE MORE disciples PODCAST

How do we make disciples at a rate that can compete with population growth, a growing secular culture, and 40% of the world considered completely unreached? With hosts, Doug Lucas of Team Expansion, Lee Wood of 1Body Church, John Heerema of Biglife, Dori Yuen of Channel Network, and special guests from around the world, we'll explore how believers can come together to make More Disciples.

MoreDisciples.com/ThePodcast

About the Author

Doug Lucas founded Team Expansion (TeamExpansion.org) in 1978 and, 45 years later, still serves as the organization's President. He has earned a bachelor's degree in Bible, a master's degree in Missions, an MBA, and a doctorate in Business Administration. Doug has been married to Penny since 1979. They have two grown sons and two granddaughters. Outside the office, Doug enjoys the 3-thirds groups he helps facilitate, playing soccer with 40 guys a lot younger than he is, playing keyboard in the worship team of his local church, and studying far-away galaxies and nebulae through the 11-inch telescope at Emerald Hills (EmeraldHillsSkies.com). Since 1995, Doug has managed Brigada, a weekly resource for missionaries, and his first book, More Disciples, is designed to help believers discover how they and their believing communities can be more effective at multiplying disciples and churches. Team Expansion makes its home on a 61-acre prayer, retreat, and learning center in Louisville, Kentucky. It currently has more than 300 full-time workers in 50 countries who pray daily that God helps them make and multiply disciples among the unreached for His glory.